"SUNWARD by YEOWARD"

This book is one of a

Limited Edition of 1000

commissioned to commemorate the

Centenary of YEOWARD BROTHERS.

....
A. R. Yeoward, Chairman   Copy No : 162

Sunward *by* Yeoward

The story of Yeoward of Liverpool – the first 100 years

Theodore W. S. Barry

Granta Editions

© Yeoward Brothers Ltd, 1994

Published by Granta Editions, 25–27 High Street,
Chesterton, Cambridge CB4 1ND, Great Britain.

Granta Editions is an imprint of Book Production Consultants Plc.

All rights reserved. No part of this publication may be reproduced, stored in any retrieval system or transmitted in any form or by any means electronic, photocopying, recording or otherwise, without the prior written permission of the copyright holder for which application should be addressed in the first instance to the publishers. No liability shall attach to the author, the copyright holder or the publishers for loss or damage of any nature suffered as a result of reliance on the reproduction of any of the contents of this publication or any errors or omission in its content.

A CIP catalogue record is available for this book from the British Library.

ISBN 1 85757 016 2

The map on page 46 has been supplied by George Philip & Son Ltd.
Permission for use of photographs/illustrations on pages 6, 19, 33, 48 and 99 given by Paul Lund and Harry Ludlam.
All other illustrations have been provided by Yeoward Brothers Ltd.

Designed by Peter Dolton.
Design and production in association with Book Production Consultants Plc, 25–27 High Street, Chesterton, Cambridge CB4 1ND, Great Britain.

Printed and bound in Singapore.

Dedication

This book is dedicated to those many thousands, and their spouses, who have faithfully served and been members of the "YEOWARD FAMILY", both at home and overseas, in many cases during their entire working lives, thus helping to enable this centenary successfully to be achieved.

It is especially dedicated to the memory of Joe Wardle, George Simpson and Geoff Jones, without whose selfless dedication, enthusiasm and support to each successive generation our jobs would not exist today.

Acknowledgements

The Yeoward Group wish to thank Nigel Watson for his contribution to the writing of this history and for the considerable research he undertook into the history of the Group.

The Group would also wish to thank Professor P N Davies, Department of Economic History at Liverpool University for his assistance.

Contents

Chapter One: 1894 – 1900 1

Chapter Two: 1900 – 1916 9

Chapter Three: 1916 – 1939 37

Chapter Four: 1939 – 1945 69

Chapter Five: 1945 – 1959 83

Chapter Six: 1959 – 1979 97

Chapter Seven: 1979 – 1989 121

Chapter Eight: 1989 and Onward 133

Epilogue 146

Appendix: Yeoward Line Fleet List 147

Family Tree 150

Index 152

chapter one

1894–1900

ON Monday, 1 January 1894, the Firm of
YEOWARD BROTHERS
opened for business in Liverpool for the first time. A century later, New Year's Day would not even be considered as a suitable date to open a new business. But in 1894 living conditions were different in many ways to what they are nowadays. Queen Victoria was still on the throne, after more than half a century, reigning over the British Empire and the world's leading power, a situation which existed not by mere coincidence but as a result of the initiative, resilience and downright hard work of a nation, with little or no social security benefits for those unable or unwilling to do their share.

In fact the peak of Victorian economic prosperity had been reached in the early 1870s. In the intervening twenty years, the national and world economy had been going through a severe depression, with several financial crises and only brief periods of relative calm; therefore the general outlook on the part of businessmen at that period was one of pessimism and fear of even worse to come.

For generations the Yeoward family had been connected with shipping, and Richard, then in his late twenties, had spent several years away from his Liverpool home operating Yeoward & Co., a shipbroker's business, in Lime St. Square in the City of London. The time had come when he felt that his ambition could no longer be satisfied thus and so in the summer of 1893 he grasped the opportunity to talk over the possibility of going into partnership with Lewis, his younger and only brother in a family of seven, with whom he enjoyed a close relationship. Meanwhile, Lewis had remained closer to home, being a partner in Green & Yeoward, a Liverpool firm of fruit wholesalers with offices in Exchange Buildings.

So it was that throughout the ensuing autumn Richard spent many weekends visiting his brother, who lived in Waterloo in the northern outskirts of Liverpool, planning with him the new partnership which was destined to change their lives out of all previous recognition and discussing it with their cousin John Pedder, a partner in the already-important firm of Liverpool solicitors, Weightman Pedder & Co., now Weightman Rutherfords and still the Company's solicitors a century later. Similarly, Hodgson Morris & Co. continue to be the Company's accountants after a whole century.

The Yeoward family had roots in Liverpool certainly as far back as the late eighteenth century and there were parallels in the previous generation to the relationship the brothers were proposing. Richard himself was following in his father's footsteps, for William Yeoward had also been a shipbroker. He had set up business as Yeoward & Co. at an office in Tithebarn Street in Liverpool in 1855, when he was twenty-seven years of age. William's younger brother, Joseph, had eventually entered the Firm in 1865, when its offices were at India Buildings, but he died at the age of only thirty-seven in 1871. By the time William died in 1890, he was acting as a merchant as well as a shipbroker.

Richard and Lewis had both had the opportunity to work apart on their own account before deciding to establish a business together. This seems to have made their partnership so much stronger and it lasted without rancour until Lewis's untimely death in the spring of 1916.

So on Saturday, 9 December, Richard closed the doors of Yeoward & Co., and departed for Liverpool. Did the two brothers have remarkable foresight, to swim against the tide of general opinion, or were they just lucky? The truth probably lies somewhere between these two extremes for it can be seen that they came in at the trough of the depression and almost immediately found themselves participating in a wave of economic optimism which was to continue until the outbreak of the Great War another twenty years later.

The solid foundation which was laid from the very outset was to be achieved only by the most rigid application of their highest moral integrity, regardless of the short-term implications for their business. Their word was truly their bond.

The driving force was quite clearly Richard, three years older than his brother. Naturally the two would pool their individual experience, of shipping and of fruit, but the influence of Richard, backed by the long family history of connection with the shipping business, dictated that this aspect would be the principal line of development for the new venture. They would combine their expertise and create a business which would deal with the chartering of vessels, the shipment of fruit from the countries of origin within those vessels, the importation of the fruit into the United Kingdom and its wholesale distribution.

Richard Joseph Yeoward (1864-1937), Founding Partner of Yeoward Brothers.

They had realised that the market for fruit in the United Kingdom was a valuable one. At the end of the nineteenth century Britain, as an industrialised nation with a large population, had become more and more dependent upon imported foodstuffs. By the 1890s a rise in real wages saw an increasing demand from a growing population for, amongst other things, more fruit and more vegetables. In 1894, the first year of trading for Yeoward Brothers, the value of apples, pears, cherries and grapes imported into the country exceeded £2,700,000, and it was an expanding market.

The brothers had agreed that, of necessity, it would be Lewis's expertise in the fruit trade which would initially provide the business's main source of income until Richard had time to develop the shipping activity. So for the first couple of years Lewis, who was already married, would be entitled to two-thirds of the profits of the new business. Thereafter, and following Richard's marriage, they would share the results equally.

With its large population and the hinterland of the industrial North-West, Liverpool presented an attractive entry point for imported fruit. It was the second greatest port, after London, not only in Britain but in the whole British Empire and the focus of the great industrial county of Lancashire's considerable import and export trade. With sixty-five docks, occupying a river frontage of six-and-a-half miles, having a water area of over six hundred acres and surrounded by thirty-six miles of quay, Liverpool also possessed excellent railway facilities for the distribution of goods countrywide, as well as any number of local hauliers, whose horse-carts and waggons covered a more immediate area.

Profits were not easy to achieve in the initial period of the new Partnership because of the uncertain seasonal nature of the business, and the brothers had to work hard to achieve success. Bertha Evans, Richard's fiancée, wrote to him from Wimbledon in March 1895 that she was sorry to hear that "you had a bad debt last week. ... But it was fortunate that you had a fairly good week to cover it. I am sorry the onion season does not promise to be a good one, dear, because I know you generally reckon upon that as paying well."

In those early days, onions were the principal commodity the brothers handled and they quickly developed an export business for the vegetable. In 1894 during their first summer, Lewis had spent six weeks in the United States developing links with American customers, an indication not only of the

Lewis Herbert Yeoward (1867-1916), Founding Partner of Yeoward Brothers.

determined effort that the brothers were putting into the business but also of the world-wide nature of the trade which they were eager to exploit.

By early 1895 the Firm was already "busy with bananas", as Bertha mentioned in another letter to Richard. As late as the 1880s there had still been no organised banana trade in the United Kingdom. Only small and irregular shipments arrived and the fruit was considered an expensive luxury. But now this was changing, largely thanks to Alfred Jones, of the Elder Dempster Line, who started to carry small quantities of the fruit from the Canary Islands on his vessels returning home from West Africa. Finding resistance from the usual sales outlets, he had solved the problem by giving the new fruit free to the costermongers who piled them high on their barrows, selling them for whatever they would fetch as they shouted their wares around the streets of Liverpool, London and Bristol. This paid off and the costermongers' barrows gave way to fruit brokers and auctions but, while there was an increasing demand for bananas in London and Liverpool and their hinterlands, the fruit still remained scarce and expensive elsewhere at the turn of the century. Richard and Lewis Yeoward, of course, were aware of all these developments. They believed that the trend would be for more and more bananas to be imported into the country as they became more generally known. They also recognised that there were very few others involved in the banana trade at that time. More importantly, they knew that the limiting factor until then had been transport – the inability of shipping to carry the fruit to its destination in sound condition and that, even then, the only transport available was on passing vessels which failed to offer a regularity of service. Put simply, here was a profitable opportunity, with a market still in its infancy, uncrowded with few competitors, with a bright future ready for entrepreneurs to make their mark.

Richard in particular was determined to visit the source of supply for himself as soon as possible; the only complicating factor was his impending marriage to Bertha on 8 June 1895.

Bertha wanted them to have a quiet honeymoon in Switzerland. Richard's reply was robust:

I was most interested to read of your suggestion that we should travel to Interlaken, which sounds a lovely idea. However, if you would like to come with me, I shall be boarding a ship in Southampton to sail to a place called the Canary Islands – if you don't know where they are, I suggest that you look them up in your atlas.

The ship Richard referred to was owned by the Union Castle Line and through his dealings with the Line, Richard had established a personal friendship with several of their staff. Indeed, he had asked Bertha to invite to the wedding the captain of the ship he was intending to take to the Islands.

Thus it came as a disappointment to him to learn that the captain's sailing had been advanced to 7 June, so on 9 May he wrote to Bertha telling her that the date of the wedding should be advanced to 6 June. But Bertha did not yield easily. The wedding date could not be changed, she protested. All the invitations had been printed and the bridesmaids could not be disappointed. She suggested that the trip to the Canaries could be postponed. A visit to Interlaken would be much more preferable and "really seems a more suitable trip for a honeymoon instead of being on a crowded steamer. Everyone is of the opinion that a trip of that description is a funny choice, dear." Nevertheless, if Richard was "so bent on going" to the Canaries, she would be willing to go but only on a convenient boat after 8 June. Richard acquiesced, although after all the arrangements had been made for the wedding, at St. Mary's Church, Wimbledon and just days before it was to take place, a telegram arrived, advising a shipment of 1,753 bunches of bananas, whereupon Lewis jokingly suggested that the wedding be postponed so that Richard could help to handle the bananas. However, not for the first time nor the last, Richard had his way and left Lewis to look after the bananas whilst he and Bertha, happily married, eventually left for the Canaries on 15 June by steamer from Liverpool.

  The Canary Islands where Richard Yeoward and his young bride landed in June 1895 were very different from those of today. They were known in shipping circles as a convenient place to stop and collect coal and fresh water, and as a maritime "crossroads" of the shipping routes, east round South Africa to India and beyond, and west to South America. Furthermore, the Islands had long enjoyed links with the British Isles (culturally and commercially very much closer than those with mainland Spain, despite forming an integral part of that country), both originally as a new home for refugees from the oppression of Oliver Cromwell, and latterly through the establishment of trade links based on their subtropical agricultural economy. The farming activity of the Islands had always been a near-monoculture, at different times based upon wine (as mentioned by Shakespeare), sugar, and cochineal. But even a third of a century after Admiral Nelson had been defeated at the naval battle of Santa Cruz, the population of the largest town in the Canary Islands amounted to a mere 8,000 people and that was only fifty years before the arrival of Richard and his bride.

  By the latter part of the century the population had expanded but the economy, still dependent almost exclusively upon primitive agriculture, had been thrown into one of its periodically recurring crises which always seemed to appear whenever the monoculture currently in fashion had come up against problems. The Islands were only just emerging from the worst economic depression in their modern history. The long-established Canary wine industry was attempting a recovery after being ravaged by a vicious vine disease in the 1850s. The Islands' major industry since the late 1820s had been the cultivation of the tiny cochineal bug for the dye industry. At its peak in 1869 cochineal worth nearly £800,000 had been exported to London. By then, however, most of the world's aniline dyes had been discovered although they were not yet in commercial production. As this developed over the following twenty years, the Islands' economy gradually collapsed.

After spending some time in Las Palmas, the principal port, situated in the island of Gran Canaria, Richard and his bride embarked on a small coaster and crossed to the neighbouring island of Tenerife, the largest of the seven main islands which make up the archipelago. Sailing along its northern coast they disembarked in the tiny fishing port of Puerto Orotava, years later to be renamed Puerto de la Cruz. The port is situated at the foot of the beautiful Valley of Orotava, from which the majestic Mount Teide rises to an impressive 12,192 feet above sea level. The principal town in the valley is La Orotava, which is itself a thousand feet above sea level. Much of the lower part of the valley at that time was planted with a wide range of different kinds of crops, none of which being obviously predominant. Naturally there were still plenty of cacti, which had been the home of the little cochineal bugs, surprisingly white in colour despite being the source of the red dye. There were also quite a number of almond trees with potatoes, maize, sundry vegetables, a few stone fruits and just the occasional banana plant all in evidence and all destined mainly for the direct consumption of their owners.

Bananas themselves were first recorded several thousand years ago in south-east Asia, from where traders had carried them through India to Africa and eventually to the Canary Islands. It was from the Islands that Columbus had carried them to America just four centuries before Richard and Bertha's visit. Thus throughout locally recorded history, bananas had always existed in the Canary Islands, although the rural population had looked upon them as an attractive decorative plant with the advantage of occasionally producing a bunch of edible fruit which would add some variety to their basic diet. But in view of the distance of the Canary Islands from any potential overseas market, that had represented the full extent of their usefulness – the visiting British traders had come to buy and ship wine, but never would they have been interested commercially in bananas, which would ripen and become useless within days.

There are over four hundred varieties of bananas known in the world. That commonly known as the "Canary banana" is the Musa Cavendishii, or Dwarf Cavendish banana, a small, delicate and easily bruised fruit. Typically, the Dwarf Cavendish banana plant grows to between twelve and fifteen feet in height, with some thirty-six leaves, and produces a single bunch per plant. The trunk is not solid, consisting merely of the tightly rolled leaves around the developing bunch before this is "born", when it emerges from the top of the roll. The bunch hangs to one side because of its own weight, and when mature will average around twenty-five to thirty kilos. It consists of about a dozen "hands", with a total of approximately one hundred and fifty individual bananas, each some six inches in length and one-and-a-half in diameter. The plant has extraordinary stability considering its exclusively-shallow rooting system. Its reproduction is from side-shoots from the base and unless these are correctly controlled by pruning, the plant will "walk" across the terrace, eventually colliding with its neighbour! Translating from the Spanish terms, the side-shoot is the "son", which grows to become the plant, known as the "mother", which "gives birth" to the bunch – perhaps the only known example of a "son" "giving birth"! It is also said that growers used to try hard to improve upon natural science and achieve "perpetual motion" by feeding the chopped-up rolls or stems to their cattle, obtaining natural fertiliser from the rear end, to put back onto the land and thereby produce another plant, which was eventually fed back into the front end etc., etc., and periodically the growers would remove the by-product – the bunch of fruit!

Apart from the more traditional honeymoon activities (which could not have included very many sightseeing excursions because there were no means of overland travel or communication), Richard occupied his time by speculating that *if* he were to purchase some land, and *if* this were to be planted with bananas, and *if* the cultivation were successful, and *if* transport facilities were available, and *if* a market could be opened up, and *if* remunerative prices could be obtained, and *if* etc., etc. … There were indeed many interdependent "*if*"s, but it was worth a try. After all, he reasoned, the local economy, even more than that of the rest of the world, was in recession and was looking for a new lead and as such would be inclined to copy any idea if this could be proved successful. Here was the germ of a possibility of creating a demand for a new shipping service, both to import those materials needed for cultivation and packing, not available locally, and subsequently to export the fruit to overseas markets. A two-way shipping service, bringing timber for packaging from Scandinavia (a trade with which he already had contacts) and marketing the fruit in the UK through the new partnership. Who knows where it might extend to as business develops? Yes, it all seemed to be a reasonable proposition.

And while he was busy in the Islands with all these plans, Richard did not overlook the need to assure the future succession – thence was their eldest son and heir conceived.

Raymond Richard Yeoward first saw the light of day, back in England, on 8 April 1896. He was destined to carry the entire responsibility for the continuation of the Yeoward family business and the employment it would provide for many other families' breadwinners through the difficult times to come in the first half of the new century.

When Richard and Bertha returned home to Liverpool, there was a great deal for the two brothers to discuss and many new plans to be made for what was already becoming a remarkably dynamic partnership. During Richard's absence Lewis had been busy and the fruit business was expanding and successful. Now with the prospect of regular and increasing supplies of bananas a distinct possibility for the not-too-distant future, they decided that it was already time to expand their base in England. Thus that same autumn they opened a fruit branch in Covent Garden, London, on 22 October 1895, at premises in Mercers Avenue, under the management of W. P. Callaghan. Thereafter it made a consistently profitable contribution to the Liverpool business.

By the time the Firm was five years old it was really humming with activity as Richard brought to the forefront his experience of shipping. They had been chartering ships to build up their trade between Liverpool and the Canary Islands and had opened a branch in Las Palmas, while in Tenerife they had appointed local agents until they opened their own branch in Santa Cruz at the beginning of the new century. Initially the business in the Canary Islands operated under the English name of "Yeoward Brothers", but this was soon translated to "Yeoward Hermanos". Locally, however, it soon became popularly known as "Casa Yeoward" (House of Yeoward).

As has already been mentioned, in England the national economy was steeped in pessimism following some twenty years of difficulties, marked by very many bankruptcies and business failures. In the Canary Islands it was worse, with many of the local population living in abject poverty and having no chance whatsoever of finding paid work nor indeed any other source of income with which to feed themselves. Many despaired of these conditions and chose to emigrate in the hope of a better way of life overseas. There was therefore no shortage of potential staff for "Casa Yeoward" and the brothers were able to set a high standard in the employees they hired.

The first executive manager to be appointed in the Canary Islands was Frederick Edward Fisher, as manager in Las Palmas. He was an energetic man who developed a reputation for being a hard task-master but one who achieved results, both in shipping and in the tomato cultivation activities which would be developed under his managership during the next three decades.

In Liverpool and London the business of Yeoward Brothers had made a successful start during the 1890s. As a fruit merchant the Firm acted as a fruit shipper, an importer and a wholesaler, and the fruit which the Firm merchanted contributed the larger part of its profits between 1894 and 1898. During the same period Yeoward also received fruit on consignment from growers, which it sold for a commission plus a handling charge. The Firm's presence in the Canary Islands and the commencement of its own shipping service was to establish Yeoward as a major importer and to have a substantial effect on earnings.

chapter two

1900–1916

FOR more than half a century the distinctive profile and colours of the Yeoward Line's steamships were well-known at both ends of the regular route the ships plied between Liverpool and the Canary Islands, calling at Lisbon and Madeira on the way. It was said that you could tell the day of the week from sighting a Yeoward steamer in the Mersey. In the Canary Islands, the name Yeoward featured in a folksong from Las Palmas, called "*El Tartanero*" about a man who has a "*tartana*", or horse-drawn coach, for sightseeing around the town. At one point in the song, the Spanish words tell that "Today the *Castle* is here, and tomorrow the *Yeoward* will arrive". The *Castle* refers to the regular arrival each week of the Union Castle mailship, which called at the Canaries en route from Southampton to South Africa. The *Yeoward*, of course, was the weekly visit to the Islands of the Yeoward steamship. Locally the name "Yeoward" came to mean a ship, any ship, in the same way that, in the English language, a "Hoover" became synonymous with a vacuum cleaner and "Biro" with a ballpoint pen.

Although the first three vessels which Richard and Lewis Yeoward bought for the Yeoward Line in 1900, 1901 and 1903, were all second-hand steamers, they had in common both their previous owner and their builder. The Cork Steamship Co. Ltd. had been the first owner of the *Avocet*, the *Fulmar*, and the *Egret*. These vessels had been built in 1885, 1888 and 1890 respectively, by W. B. Thompson & Co. Ltd. (known as the Caledon Shipbuilding & Engineering Company from 1896), whose Dundee shipyard had opened in 1874. The brothers were so taken by the name of the first vessel, the *Avocet*, that they decided that all their ships should in future bear the names of birds, and furthermore that they should all commence with the letter A. So the *Fulmar* and the *Egret* became the *Ardeola* and the *Avetoro* respectively. Subsequently, it was decided that they would be more distinctive if henceforth they should not only commence, but also terminate, with the same letter A, so that *Avetoro* became the only exception. The brothers were also so pleased with the performance of their first three ships that, except when wartime necessitated the further purchase of second-hand vessels, all

The first Yeoward Line steamer, s.s. Avocet, entering Liverpool Docks in early 1900. Note the heavy sparred sailing ships in the background.

future steamers of the Yeoward Line were ordered from the Dundee yard of the Caledon Shipbuilding & Engineering Company.

The *Avocet*, the *Ardeola* and the *Avetoro* were all vessels of between 1,000 and 1,200 tons and had been designed principally as cargo vessels, although they had limited accommodation for a dozen passengers. The *Avocet*, for example, had cargo space of nearly 77,000 cubic feet on its two lower decks, reached through five deck hatches. It was the passenger aspect, however, which was to be the forerunner of one of the most significant developments in the early history of the Firm – the extension of their shipping business to the carriage of passengers. All three vessels proved a great success on the Canary run and the brothers decided in the autumn of 1903 to place an order for the Yeoward Line's first purpose-built steamer from the Caledon yard. The intention was for this to be the Line's fourth vessel but, on 10 December 1903, the *Ardeola*, under the command of Capt. McCracken, was involved in a collision with a sailing vessel and sank in the Bay of Biscay while homeward-bound from Las Palmas. All hands were rescued but the

1900–1916

Left: Typical banana plantation in Tenerife.

Below: Typical development of a banana plant showing the "son" born from the "mother" plant. See page 7.

Above: s.s. Ardeola – the first purpose-built steamer of the Yeoward Line – 1904.

Right: Yeoward Line Post Card – 1913.

costly navigational error spelt the end of Capt. McCracken's career with the Yeoward Line. The new steamer, handed over by the yard in the summer of 1904, thus became the Yeoward Line's second *Ardeola*.

This purpose-built vessel, at £22,500, cost almost twice as much as the average of the prices paid for the first three ships. She was the first Yeoward liner to sport the distinctive features which were to make the Yeoward ships so easily recognisable – the grey-painted hull with the high white-painted freeboard, the three raked masts and the lofty funnel set between the main and the mizzen. The funnel was black with a central band painted in the Line's adopted Spanish colours of red, yellow and red, the single letter Y being picked out in black on the yellow band.

The new *Ardeola*'s cargo space was comparable with her predecessor's, three-quarters of it well forward from the engine-room, ensuring her delicate cargo would not be spoilt by too much heat. More important, however, was the greater emphasis upon passenger accommodation which gave her the capability of catering for passengers in great comfort. And the most important innovation of all was the basic concept of marketing this passenger accommodation. Until then, most ship operators worldwide had tended to look upon passengers, like cargo, as clients who wished to travel from one point to another, especially so to and from the Canary Islands where both passengers and cargo were accommodated if and when space was available on passing ships. Now the Islands would enjoy a service designed specifically for them and with regularity of service throughout the year. The first "cruises" from Liverpool to the Canary Islands and back, for a duration

Three ships of the Yeoward Line.

of twenty-one days and at a price of six guineas, were on the new *Ardeola*. As early as 1903 the following advertisement appeared:

Canary Islands

Yeoward Bros. Line

The following first-class steamers are despatched from the Coburg Dock, Liverpool, taking passengers for Santa Cruz de Teneriffe and Las Palmas, Grand Canary.

Saloon Fare (inclusive)
Six Guineas, single, Ten Guineas, return

Steamers usually call at Lisbon on the outward voyage, and holders of return tickets may land at any port of call, and resume their voyage at any time convenient with the sailings of the steamers.

S.S. *Avocet* 1,219 tons 100.A1 at Lloyd's Capt. McClean
S.S. *Ardeola* 1,204 tons 100.A1 at Lloyd's Capt. McCracken

Bathrooms, Electric Light, etc.

Hotel Accommodation in the Islands from 2 guineas per week.

What was more, with typical foresight and business acumen, Richard had made travelling by the Yeoward Line even more attractive by arranging for passengers to book their hotel accommodation in advance at the same time as they booked their passage. In fact, all of the relatively few hotels and boarding houses which existed in those early days agreed special rates for the Yeoward passengers. The "package tour" had been introduced. It was this initiative which provoked Elder Dempster to retaliate with a "holiday ticket" which included two weeks' accommodation and board at the Hotel Metropole in Las Palmas together with the return voyage.

But even this did not wrest the initiative away from Richard. The new *Ardeola* came equipped with twelve staterooms which, with their double bunk berths and a sofa-bed as an occasional extra berth, could accommodate up to thirty-six passengers, as many as the first three Yeoward steamers put together. Yet

Embarking passengers, Prince's Landing Stage, Liverpool.

Above: Launch of the "Aguila".

Left, bottom left and below: Typical interior of a Yeoward vessel 1913.

s.s. Andorinha returning home during her maiden voyage – 1911.

The third Ardeola on her maiden voyage 1912 anchored off Las Palmas. Signed by Richard Yeoward, Capt. Prendergast and other passengers and crew.

within seven years she had been sold because she was no longer large enough for Yeoward's expanding passenger business. Three more new steamers were delivered to the Yeoward Line before 1914, each larger and more luxurious than its predecessor. The Line paid £34,000 for the *Aguila* of 1909. She carried a maximum of nearly one hundred passengers in her thirty-two staterooms, a striking indication of how attractive the Yeoward Line was proving to be with passengers. She had an elegant dining saloon, a smoke room for the gentlemen and a music room complete with piano. The *Andorinha* of 1911, an agile liner with a coquettish air, was the first Yeoward liner to be fitted with wireless telegraphy. For the sum of £40,000, she came with thirty-one staterooms and two even more luxurious de luxe cabins. The third *Ardeola*, delivered in 1912, was the first Yeoward steamer of more than 3,000 tons. At a cost of £50,000, she was the most opulently fitted passenger ship in the fleet of five liners. She had thirty-eight staterooms and two de luxe cabins, while part of her extra space was given over to the provision of a saloon and

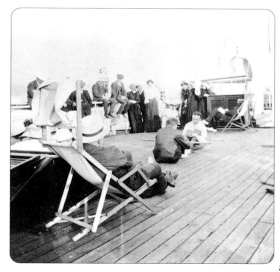

library in addition to other public rooms previous ships had provided. Because of one of her seagoing traits, the *Ardeola* became known affectionately as the "Hardyroller"!

In the minds of many people, the ships of the Yeoward Line soon became identified not with bananas but with cruising, under the slogan "**Sunward by Yeoward**". It was this idea which Richard seized upon. The superior passenger accommodation of the second *Ardeola* enabled the Yeoward Line to publicise round-trip cruises of twenty-two days for ten guineas return. By 1913 the return ticket on a Yeoward cruise liner still cost only ten guineas on the two oldest steamers, the *Avocet* and the *Avetoro*, which had already proved their attraction with passengers. For a premium of another four guineas, a passage could be had upon the *Aguila*, the *Andorinha* and the third *Ardeola*, modern vessels and all equipped to the highest standard for the carriage of first-class passengers. Would-be passengers were tempted to take a Yeoward cruise by the elegant, colourful, and well-designed posters found at railway stations and elsewhere around the country and by the beguiling descriptions of the cruises contained in the Firm's brochures. One such brochure, an attractive 97-page booklet, was the delightful *A Letter Home* of 1913. Written in the style of a letter, it is only after several pages that the reader realises what a magnificent, subtle and attractive piece of advertising the brochure is. *A Letter Home*, supposedly written by a passenger on board the *Andorinha*, boasted of "an air of quiet and good taste" aboard the vessel, reflected, for example, in "the passengers dressing for dinner, as is customary on all the best liners". But it also described the many opportunities for relaxation which passengers enjoyed on board. There were deck games like "cock fighting", deck cricket, pillow fighting astraddle a spar and egg and spoon races. Excursions were arranged at every port of call. In Lisbon, for example, a tour of the city

"Cock Fighting" on board the s.s. Andorinha, May/June 1911.

Deck sports.

sunward by yeoward

Top: Passengers on the maiden voyage of the s.s. Andorinha, May/June 1911, enjoying a picnic at Orotava.

The "Last Lament" – s.s. Andorinha 1911.

was followed by a night spent at Mont Estoril. In Orotava, passengers were able to visit the largest of Yeoward Brothers' banana farms. The peace and quiet, the periods of hearty exercise, the warmth of the sun and the delights of the Islands meant that "we have no invalids or semi-invalids amongst us now after our health-giving journey".

As was the custom in those days, each ship was constituted as a single company. In the five separate steamship companies representing the *Avocet*, *Avetoro*, *Ardeola*, *Aguila*, and *Andorinha*, the families of Richard and Lewis held slightly less than 50% each, while a handful of shares were distributed amongst senior employees or close friends or relatives. The total capitalisation of the various companies which made up the Yeoward Line by 1914 was £120,000 and almost all that capital had been raised by the family itself.

The Firm of Yeoward Brothers acted as the steamship managers for each of the ship-owning companies, for which it received a management fee, which in 1914 was 5% of the gross income of each ship company, having steadily increased upon the acquisition of every new ship. By that period the Yeoward Line was earning a total income of approximately £150,000 per year from their combined carriage of passengers and freight.

As the Firm expanded in all directions, its offices in Liverpool at 27 and 29 Stanley Street (to which it had moved in 1901) became progressively more and more cramped, until in 1912 it had become virtually impossible to continue with them as the Head Office. Thus Harvey Buildings, 25 James Street, in the heart of the shipping centre of the city of Liverpool, was bought as the Firm's new Head Office. Harvey Buildings was a typical example of the classic architecture of the city built in the latter half of the 19th century when the city was enjoying great prosperity, with noble materials such as solid mahogany and marble.

Several departments were established there covering various aspects of the shipping business: freight, cartage, passengers, victualling and the marine and engineers' department. In addition, the Firm had its own export department which was engaged principally in processing orders obtained by the Canary Island branches for shipment on the Yeoward steamers. The branches in turn acted as sales agents in the Islands for such commodities as

chemical fertilisers, seed potatoes, tomato seed and packing materials. Progressively, passenger and cargo agents were appointed throughout the United Kingdom.

Meanwhile, the increasing business of shipping and related activities on land had required the provision of more adequate facilities on shore in the Canaries. This could not be handled personally by either Richard or Lewis Yeoward, busy men thousands of miles – and a week's journey – away. There is no evidence that Lewis ever visited the Islands, while Richard's visits were infrequent. Indeed, his last visit to the Canaries was in 1912, seventeen years before he retired from the business. Nor was it possible for anyone else at Head Office in Liverpool to keep anything more than a distant oversight upon matters in the Islands. Instead, it was the policy of the brothers from the beginning to appoint executive managers from the United Kingdom, send them out to the Canaries and entrust them with a substantial degree of independence in the running of the business.

The Yeoward Brothers offices at Harvey Buildings, James Street in Liverpool c. 1912-41.

The brothers were generally well-served by those they appointed. The first manager to be sent out to the Canaries was Frederick Fisher who, as has already been related, opened their first Canary branch in Las Palmas de Gran Canaria in 1899. He arranged the purchase of a central site on which the Firm built its offices. This was expanded when two adjoining sites were added, for warehouses and garaging. Soon afterwards, a convenient office building was also acquired in Santa Cruz de Tenerife for a new branch recently established there under Maurice Smith, who continued until his death there in active service in 1938. An elegant and well-

Yeoward offices in Las Palmas – 1911.

educated man with a polished personality and a quiet and retiring disposition, Smith came with considerable experience of working in ports along the west coast of South America. He became well-known at the British Club in Santa Cruz, where he was known as "Yeoward Smith" to distinguish him from "Bank Smith" who worked for the local branch of the Bank of British West Africa.

Puerto Orotava, showing former Yeoward offices as the white building – 1913.

**Top: The Mole, Icod.
Centre: Surfboat shipping bananas, Orotava.**

Frank Artus, the same age as Lewis, became the first manager in Puerto Orotava, which was situated half-way along the north coast of Tenerife and where trading commenced in October 1899. He enjoyed the full authority of the partners, and a great deal of autonomy which he was destined to use to the great benefit of "Casa Yeoward". He had a strong and respected personality and integrated fully into local society. Although merely a tiny fishing village, Puerto Orotava was officially considered as a principal port, having its own Customs, Port Health and Port Authority. Sometimes there would be as many as six steamers or sailing vessels anchored off its tiny jetty. Initially an office was established overlooking the port but soon afterwards the Firm moved to Casa de la Real Aduana, the old customs house on the side of the little port and they subsequently rented the house for several years to come.

Overland communications were still extremely restricted at the turn of the century, with most transport going by sea around the coast. It was because of this problem that Richard and Lewis bought the small steam ketch, *Stefanie* (which they renamed *Alca*) in 1904, from a German firm for inter-island and coastal transport and opened a number of sub-branches in coastal villages such as Garachico in 1908. There were several occasions when the *Alca* touched bottom in the rocky coastlines of Puerto Orotava and Garachico without mishap and her old Captain, Robert Milhench, was well-known for his favourite saying: "*Alca* breaks rocks – rocks do not break *Alca*". In his earlier days Capt. Milhench had commanded some of the heaviest sparred sailing vessels out of Liverpool, in the days of "ships of wood – men of iron", which in his opinion had then changed to "ships of iron – men of wood". Years later the Spanish authorities obliged the Firm to re-register the coaster under the Spanish flag and to employ a Spanish captain. Alcohol was getting the better of Capt. Milhench by that time and he was sent as relieving officer on one of the Yeoward steamers, under Capt. Donald McPhee. Nowhere was there a man more intolerant of drink than Capt. McPhee so out went "Old Bob", as Capt. Milhench was known.

The Canary Island branches were engaged variously in fruit production, in securing consignments, as agents for the Yeoward Line steamers, as stevedores and as general traders, mainly through the growing and packing of fruit for export by Yeoward ships. "Casa Yeoward" handled not only its own banana production but also fruit and vegetables on consignment from various other growers and shippers in the Islands. Many of these growers benefited from the financial support given by "Casa Yeoward", often in cash, sometimes in kind, by the supply of materials on credit and usually in advance of the season's harvest to ease cashflow problems.

Yeoward Brothers offices at Orotava c. 1915.

Quay-side scene in the Canaries on the maiden voyage of the s.s. Andorinha, 1911.

Their three able managers were the most important men in "Casa Yeoward" at this time but even they began to feel the need for assistance as the business grew steadily before the Great War. As the branch at the heart of the Yeoward Brothers' banana farms, it was Orotava which needed most strengthening. In 1911 Frank Artus was joined by William Clark and, in the following year, by Alfred Brabyn. Clark came from the offices of Yeoward's Liverpool lawyers, Weightman Pedder, and he had the character of the driest of lawyers; but he was absolutely honest, a thorough, numerate and decisive administrator and paternal in his dealings with staff. He preferred the company of the English community and never really became integrated into the local society as had Artus, whom he succeeded on the latter's retirement in 1919. He enjoyed good relations with those locals who were well-placed socially but it was a relationship born of mutual respect rather than personal warmth or friendship and was entirely dependent on the significance of "Casa Yeoward" which he represented. Brabyn joined "Casa Yeoward" from South Africa and had the advantage of being fluent in Spanish. He had imagination and was a good organiser but was often timid. The two men were thus totally complementary, each providing what the other lacked. In Las Palmas, at about the same time, the young local Spaniard, Juan Perdomo Aguilar, jumped at Frederick Fisher's offer of employment in "Casa Yeoward", already one of the more important firms in commercial and financial circles in Las Palmas. In years to come he was to develop into a very proud man and was to rise to the position of joint manager in Las Palmas until his retirement half a century later, a post in which he enjoyed considerable prestige in his island of Gran Canaria. He was to say himself that his position was destined to give him great satisfaction in life and he proudly kept framed the letter from Fisher granting his original appointment.

During this period Frank Artus in particular can be said to have laid the foundations for "Casa Yeoward"'s considerable landholdings in the Islands, concentrated as they were in the Orotava Valley. In 1907 he formalised the earlier purchase of Casa Azul and the adjoining land of some nine *fanegadas*, equivalent to twelve acres, which would soon be developed into the Lagar farm and become the centre of Yeoward's farming operations in the Orotava Valley. Likewise, during its first forty years of existence, the Firm built up very extensive holdings of water shares, mostly by purchase, but in some cases by active participation in the creation and development of new water galleries. The large Lagar irrigation tank was constructed under Artus's managership and prior to the outbreak of the Great War he was instrumental in purchasing tracts of land which were assembled into farms known as La Paz, Rechazos, Franco and Calderina. Artus also purchased a small warehouse with adjoining sites on the main road in La Vera, near Casa Azul, which, after being burnt down during the Popular Front disturbances in 1934, was redeveloped as a modern warehouse for the central storage of farm materials, such as fertilizers, and later (1966) became the packing-house, when the Firm's original packing-house became the Town Hall.

Richard Yeoward and Bertha (on his right) enjoying a camel ride at Orotava – 1911.

Once harvested, the produce of the various farms was transported by carts pulled by mules, oxen or camels (there were no lorries until after the Great War) to the Firm's packing-house, situated on the seafront near their offices. Here the bunches of bananas were graded by size and weight, to be packed into crates wrapped in wadding, straw or old newspapers, the latter being old stock bought by the Firm from Liverpool's newspaper publishers and shipped out on the Yeoward steamers. Smaller bunches were packed two or three to a crate and, being of less value, it was not unknown for some less scrupulous shippers to fasten the bunches together in the hope that they might pass as higher grades. Tomatoes and potatoes were packed in boxes, generally in peat dust. Yeoward's own trademarks were well-known for quality in the United Kingdom; bananas were generally marked "YHL" (Lewis Yeoward's initials in reverse), while the best-known brand for their tomatoes and potatoes at that time was "COCK". The Firm also handled other similar produce on behalf of other growers for sale on commission.

Whenever the sea permitted, the Yeoward Line steamers would anchor off Puerto Orotava to unload and load cargo and passengers, using the Firm's two passenger launches and six cargo launches, each with a capacity of 9 to 10 tons. This virtually never happened during the winter months, however, when all merchandise had to be transported overland to Santa Cruz – a journey which then took twenty-four hours by way of bullock-cart to Tacorante and thence onward whenever possible by tram service to the port of Santa Cruz. The launches had been constructed by the Firm's own carpenters, on the patio of the packing-house by the wharf. In fact the largest of the cargo launches – fondly known by the seamen as the *Lorry* due to its disproportionate width – had been launched with great local ceremony with the name of *Ricardo José*, Richard Yeoward's names in Spanish. The Firm's permanent staff at that time included two foremen, a crane-driver, a marine carpenter and several others.

s.s. Andorinha anchored off Puerto Orotava in 1911.

On one occasion, while a Yeoward steamer lay anchored off Puerto Orotava busy loading crates of bananas, a sudden storm blew up, obliging the captain to order steam to be raised and the ship to sail immediately. At that moment two of the cargo launches were tied alongside and, due to the sudden change in the weather, they were unable to return safely to shore. There was no option but to take them in tow, all the way to Santa Cruz. Also, the stevedores who were working on board found themselves similarly stranded. On board it is recorded that they enjoyed plenty of good food and drink but the item which especially appealed to them, being a complete novelty, was the lettuce; "Give us more leaves!" they called, in their local dialect. For their return voyage two days later, after the storm had abated, the launches with the stevedores on board were towed back to Puerto Orotava by a sailing coaster – apparently with much less excitement!

On another occasion recorded in a report many years later, the *Ardeola* was similarly loading bananas off Puerto Orotava on 18 November 1909 when rumours started to spread through the Island that a new volcanic eruption had commenced somewhere in the mountains behind the town of Garachico, westwards along the north coast of Tenerife. Apparently there were confused scraps of information about alarm and panic, evoking memories of the volcanic eruption two centuries earlier, in 1705, when the old town had been almost wiped out by a disastrous lava flow. Even in 1909 means of communication were primitive in the extreme – in that part of the Island there were hardly any roads, and transport was either on foot or animal-drawn carts. The authorities in Santa Cruz, on the other side of the Island, faced with uncertainty, decided to call for warships to sail towards Garachico in order to evacuate the village, if this proved to be necessary. Hearing rumours of the possible danger, the captain of the *Ardeola* decided to raise anchor and sail immediately to Garachico to assist. There he anchored and waited, fortunately in vain, as no lava flow appeared and once the nerves of the population had calmed down, the *Ardeola* was able to return to Puerto Orotava to continue loading bananas for Liverpool. It was in fact later discovered that the eruption was on the other side of the mountain range, so the lava flow was to the opposite coast on the south of the Island. A present day reminder in Garachico of that incident so many years ago, is a bar named *Ardeola* with the name having been taken from an "English ship anchored off the shore".

Similarly recorded was the unfortunate experience which might merit the title "The Eleventh Commandment". The "Casa Yeoward", Fyffes and Elder Dempster were at that time the only three firms in Puerto Orotava with any commercial and accounting organisation, all based on the English system. Their local cashiers knew each other well and were good friends in the small village. Each of them would consider it normal practice to resolve the other's temporary personal financial problems with the help of his own firm's funds which he controlled, readjusting matters whenever they were better able so to do. From time to time, their firm's internal auditor would announce his intention to carry out a routine inspection. Suspicious precisely because the cash always seemed to balance, the respective auditors on one occasion combined together in setting a trap which consisted simply of carrying out their inspections simultaneously. Unable to call on either of the other cashiers for a temporary "loan" to enable his books to balance, the subterfuge was discovered and the Yeoward cashier fled to Cuba. He was a man of ability, well-versed in international commerce of the period and spoke good English. In Cuba he very soon obtained a senior position with the American Sugar Company where he prospered, becoming closely involved with the authorities and with the furtherance of American financial interests, and having at his personal disposal a detachment of the Cuban National Guard. Many years later he returned to Puerto de la Cruz on holiday and visited the office, where he repaid to Mr. Clark and Mr. Brabyn the nine thousand pesetas which had been missing (when a labourer's wages were three pesetas per day) and presented each of them with a box of Cuban cigars.

Once the Yeoward steamers had reached their berth at the North Coburg Dock in Liverpool, the fruit was unloaded from the ships and inspected by Yeoward's staff of some ten fruit selectors. It was then taken by the Firm's own horses and carts to the dockside railway depots. Yeoward always sent goods carriage paid and thus was able to claim a cartage rebate from the carriage charge made by the railways which included an element for cartage. At the dockside the Firm had extensive stabling for its horses, large warehouses for its fruit (eventually including gas heating for the protection and ripening of bananas) and the storage of other goods and two dock offices for inward and outward cargo.

Bananas were sold "almost invariably" hard and green but, when prices were poor, they were warehoused for protection, often for local buyers, sometimes on Yeoward Brothers' own account. The fruit which lay ripening in the crates had to be regularly inspected by the warehouseman. "Turning over", as it was termed, was something of an art, since judgement of condition was made by touch rather than by sight and a good warehouseman could save lots of money by his diligence and care in moving out fruit that would otherwise have quickly rotted. Quantities of bananas in warehouses were sometimes so heavy that several dockmen had to lend a hand in turning over the fruit.

Produce from other sources, in particular onions and grapes, was also warehoused in quantity. Grapes were emptied from the barrels in which they arrived and any imperfect grapes removed, to ensure the barrels were fit for re-export to the United States and Canada – important markets for the Firm at that time.

Canary produce formed only part of the Liverpool-based wholesale fruit business. This was conducted largely from the Firm's own saleroom in Victoria Street, under the direction of Lewis Yeoward. Here there were two departments: the Canary Fruit department, and the Green Fruit department which dealt with all non-Canary produce. Lewis and the Firm's general manager at this time, Edward Jones, spent much time there, especially on auction days, every Monday, Wednesday and Friday. In the period before the First World War, Lewis gradually expanded the range of produce handled by the business. There were apples from America and Australasia, onions from Egypt (where Yeoward had its own storage yard in Alexandria), oranges from Spain and Palestine, grapes from Spain and Portugal, lemons from Italy and a variety of home-grown produce. The Firm developed especially strong links with several apple- and pear-growers in Tasmania, notably Terry Brothers, and in the United States with the apple-growers Glaize Brothers of Virginia. Lewis had agents in most originating countries but did not hesitate to buy fruit in bulk at auction if direct imports were scarce and often did so at other times for quick resale, although the margins were usually very low. To generate sales, Lewis arranged the despatch of hundreds of circulars and special-offer letters to customers. Scotland was especially important for the sale of large-bunch banana crates, while the Manchester trade took many of the smaller double and treble-bunch crates. A great deal of fruit was also sold in Dublin and Belfast. While the Manchester trade could be covered from Liverpool, it was more difficult to cover other areas of the country where Yeoward Brothers had customers. In two of the most important areas of custom for Yeowards, Scotland and the North East, the success of the business enabled Richard and Lewis to open a branch in Glasgow in 1908 and another in Newcastle in 1911. Other principal markets were covered by the appointment of agents.

The Liverpool business of Yeoward Brothers was profitable over the whole of this period. Profits doubled in 1901 and remained at a similar level until 1910, when they rose another 50% to a level largely sustained until the outbreak of war. No doubt these profit improvements related to the development of the Yeoward Line and the entry into service of the *Aguila*. Not only did these two events enable the carriage of more fruit from the Canaries but they also contributed significant sums in terms of management fees to Yeoward Brothers. The bulk of the profits for the Liverpool business arose from commission and charges earned on handling consignments (nearly 60% of profits), while contributions from the Firm's bought and sold activities and steamer management fees both contributed around 10% to 15% of profits. In addition, there were variable and intermittent profits from individual fruit ventures from year to year, which could contribute as much as another £9,000 to Liverpool's profits. It is worth pointing out here that Frederick Baines, who joined Yeoward in the early 1900s in the role of insurance expert, was responsible for ensuring that the Firm minimised the risk of loss involved in its Australasian apple and pear ventures. These losses could often be crippling in such a seasonal and uncertain trade. Baines, with Yeoward's insurance brokers, introduced the "Yeoward Brothers Deterioration Clause" into the Firm's policies which, according to George Simpson, "has probably never been improved upon in giving protection against certain types of loss".

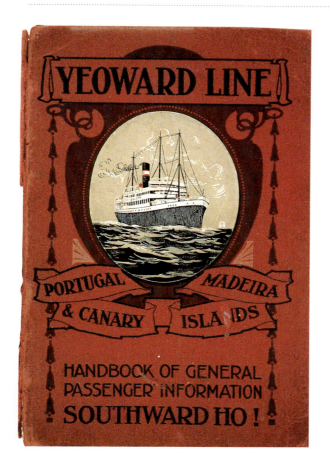

Left: Cover of early Yeoward Line cruise brochure c.1913 featuring '*A Letter Home*'.

Below: This painting showing two early Yeoward vessels was painted by the same artist responsible for the poster shown on the cover.

Typical poster used by the Yeoward Line c.1913.

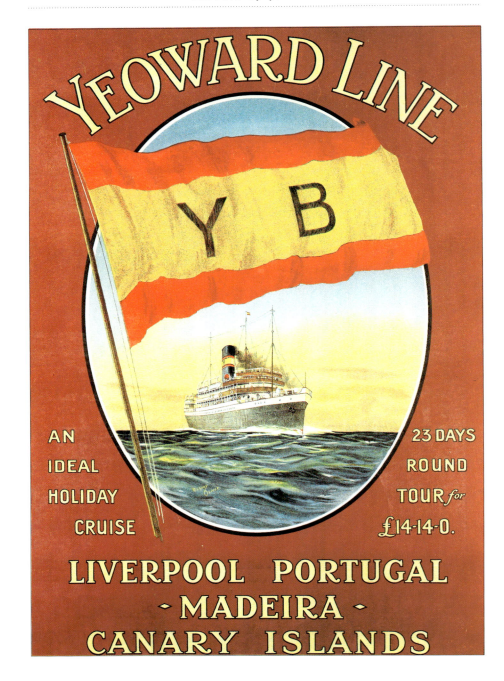

By this time the Liverpool business was making profits of around £50,000 a year, excluding both those made by the individual ship companies which made up the Yeoward Line (for which no records remain) and those of the business in the Canary Islands. Similarly, the results of the fruit branches were treated separately from those of the Liverpool business. These three branches themselves were always in profit apart from a small loss recorded by the London branch in the first half of 1914 and most of their profits arose from commission and handling charges on consignment fruit. Annual contributions from the branches were, however, small, varying between only £1,000 and £2,000 over this period. In other words, all the Yeoward businesses, in the United Kingdom, in the Canary Islands and at sea, would appear to have been very profitable. In twenty years the two brothers had built up a considerable business.

In 1911 – the year before the sinking of the unsinkable *Titanic* – the partners decided that the time had come to formalise their business relationship – although it seems more probable that, with their sons growing up, they considered it wise to provide for the future of the business. In Liverpool a "Deed of Partnership of Yeoward Brothers" was made between Richard Joseph Yeoward and Lewis Herbert Yeoward, on 11 September 1911. One of its clauses specifically authorised Lewis to bring his son Cyril into the partnership when he reached the age of twenty-five years (so presumably the facility would have been mutual, likewise authorising Richard to introduce his sons Raymond and Bernard as partners on their twenty-fifth birthdays). In practice this provision never took effect, as Lewis died five years later while Cyril was still a minor and he subsequently showed no interest in becoming involved in the Firm. Lewis, who also had one daughter, had made his Will on 15 November 1912. This foresaw the possibility that not only might his son become a partner in the Firm, but so also might any future son-in-law. There was most definitely, however, no provision for his daughter in her own right – in those days the place for a female was most certainly not in business!

In mid-July of 1914 King George V reviewed the Fleet at Spithead in what was the largest review of sea power ever seen in the British Isles either before or since. There were forty miles of ships assembled in twelve lines and, apart from Royal Navy vessels, there were also about forty merchant ships representing all the leading shipping companies. Representing the Yeoward Line that proud day was the *Aguila*, under the command of Capt. Bannerman. In reality the review was an exercise in patriotism, in preparation for the outbreak of war which, following the assassination of the Grand Duke Ferdinand of Austria, was becoming more obvious as days went by. Only two weeks later war on Germany was finally declared, and there were many people who believed that the country's famous regiments and great naval strength would bring victory before Christmas. How wrong …!

Christmas came and went and the war was not over. But neither was it having any very direct effect on the day-to-day life of the general public … yet! The year 1915 arrived and with it the arrival of the second generation into the Firm. Raymond Richard Yeoward, elder son of Richard, was now eighteen years of age.

Liverpool was a maritime city, far removed from the land war which was slowly developing in the distant continent of Europe. Until the outbreak of the Great War, there was a strong feeling of what might be termed the Brotherhood of the Sea between naval officers of all major maritime nations. First and foremost they were gentlemen and they were professional seamen. In times of war between their nations, they knew and abided by the rules and they gave and enjoyed mutual respect. They did not kill innocent seamen in cold blood; the sinking of merchant ships in the early days of the war was a relatively civilised business. The naval warship which intercepted an enemy merchant vessel would order the latter to position herself for boarding, request her captain and crew to pack their personal belongings and transfer them as prisoners of war, while sailors from the naval vessel prepared to scuttle the merchant ship either by opening sea-cocks or by placing explosives.

Only with this background in mind can later generations understand the deep sense of public outrage in Britain when it was realised that the enemy German navy had changed those rules, motivating such headlines as appeared in the press on 20 May 1915 declaring: "Callous conduct of German submarine's crew – Barbarous attack on Yeoward liner – Liner's commander and crew honoured."

German "U-boats" were starting to make their presence felt and the Admiralty had advised that some of them "were fitted with a small gun but that was really a very ineffective weapon and should be no menace to a steel ship".

Normally the Yeoward ships would sail from Liverpool on Saturdays but, on the advice of the Naval Authorities and with Richard's agreement, *Aguila*'s sailing was advanced to Friday, 27 March 1915. The next afternoon, nearing the Smalls lighthouse, a submarine appeared flying a signal "Stop and heave to or I will fire into you." At that point Capt. Bannerman was confronted with a very grave decision. Apart from sending a distress message, he had to decide whether to comply with the demands of an armed enemy vessel or attempt to evade her, bearing in mind the possible risk to life that such a decision might incur.

He turned away and increased to full speed, but to little avail; the submarine opened fire almost immediately and the first shot put a nasty gash in the captain's right arm. The helmsman jumped over the side in terror and Capt. Bannerman took over the helm himself. Chief Engineer Edwards appeared on the bridge to report that they were doing all the speed that they could and moments later he received a head wound, from which he died shortly afterwards. After about two hours of this shelling, with the steering gear put out of action, *Aguila* came to a stop and the crew prepared to leave in the lifeboats. The steward Frank James had the calm foresight to provision them with adequate supplies of spirits ...!

The submarine closed with the crippled ship which was settling by the stern but the engine room bulkhead was holding her up and the survivors had hopes of spending the night on her for they could see the beginnings of a heavy snowstorm brewing. However, the U-29 manoeuvred into position and put a torpedo into her; her bow rose up high and she quickly sank by the stern. U-29 was commanded by Kapitänleutnant Graf von Forster, who became an admiral in the Second World War. But once he had sunk his unarmed prey, he departed, abandoning the survivors in the open lifeboats to their fate.

During that Saturday night, due to the snowstorm and the darkness, the two lifeboats became separated. Capt. Bannerman's boat was found next morning by a fishing trawler from Milford Haven, to where it returned with the survivors. They landed on the Monday and were treated very well, having their wounds dressed before travelling home that same night. They were very distressed about the loss of their colleagues in the other lifeboat and next morning Capt. Bannerman went to the Liverpool office to report to Richard Yeoward. Wednesday brought the wonderful news that the other boat had been found by the Scottish steamer *Lady Plymouth* and all the large number of crew on board had been rescued. As a result of this rescue the death toll was reduced to a total of eight persons, including the sole lady passenger and the stewardess.

There was universal praise for the bravery of captain and crew and a few weeks later they were entertained by the Lord Mayor of Liverpool, who said they were there to do honour to the master, officers and crew of the mail steamer *Aguila* and to recognise their courage and devotion to their owners and their country under most difficult, perilous and trying circumstances. It was fitting that such a ceremony should take place in the Town Hall and the Lord Mayor, representing the citizens of Liverpool, said he was proud to be associated with it. He emphasised very strongly the measures which ought to be taken against Germany in the way of reprisals for her submarine attacks on non-combatant passenger liners.

Captain Bannerman, in reply, remarked that the presentations were a tremendous surprise to him and the last thing he expected. In regard to the reasons for which they were being honoured, he and his crew were merely carrying out their duty and his only regret was the loss of life which had been suffered.

The reaction of the partners to the loss of the *Aguila* was to maintain their fleet and in order to do so they would have to buy a replacement. Within some three or four months the purchase of the *Don Hugo* from Rio Tinto Co. was completed, whereupon she was renamed *Alondra* and Capt. Bannerman was appointed to command her when she was ready for service. Meanwhile, the *Avetoro* was on a six-voyage charter to Sievewright Bacons and he was asked to take her for this period while the *Alondra* was refitted. Five voyages passed uneventfully but on the sixth and last she sailed from Birkenhead to Barry to pick up an outward freight of coal destined for the Admiralty depot in Las Palmas (all British naval vessels were coal-fired at that time). She sailed on 8 November 1915, sheltering that night from a gale in the lee of Lundy Island. On 10 November she was sighted by the Allen liner *Scotian* and that was the last that was ever seen or heard of her. She had no wireless installation and was lost without trace with all hands, presumably sunk by enemy action.

At such times the Firm did not hesitate to do all possible to mitigate at least the financial hardship faced by the families of those who had died. This included the granting of generous allowances, especially in the case of widowed mothers with young children, and maintaining these allowances until long after the children had grown up. Three-quarters of a century later, it is easy to forget that social services, the "welfare state" and even pensions had scarcely been invented. It was a time when hardship was commonplace and much depended on the attitude of the employer but it is certain that generosity was less than universal. It was aspects such as these which prompted Richard to introduce the Pension Fund in the following year, a socially enlightened benefit which in those days was most uncommon.

It was only with luck that the Yeoward Line had not lost another vessel in August 1915. On two separate occasions off the south coast of Ireland, the *Avocet* had been surprised by a German submarine. On the first occasion, a submarine had attacked her with gunfire and she, then the oldest ship in the Yeoward fleet, had somehow managed to shake off the aggressor by escaping at speed. Chased by another submarine on a second occasion, she had evaded destruction by the same method. To have done so twice was quite a tribute to the qualities of the ship's chief engineer.

Meanwhile, to a very considerable extent the Canary Islands were cut off from the outside world; trade stopped and real hardship and poverty increased. The Great War also put an end to banana exportation and with the Spanish domestic market still non-existent, the coaster *Alca* was sold to a

Spanish shipowner in Bilbao. There developed a form of siege economy in the Islands where money was of necessity frequently substituted by more primitive methods. Those banana-growers who were able to do so continued to attend to their cultivations and water was plentiful although frequently the fruit produced would find no market. Thus for the minority, lucky enough to remain in employment, their wages, equivalent to two pesetas per day, were frequently paid in kind. Social security and unemployment subsidies were not even a remote dream over the horizon as quite simply they had not yet been thought of and hardship was rife. Under the personal direction of Mr. and Mrs. Artus, the Firm set up kitchens to provide free meals to the needy folk and distributed fresh milk for the children and the sick. Supplies of food were brought into the Islands on rare visits which the Yeoward Line steamers were able to make and distributed free to all those who were in need.

Head Office sent substantial sums to finance the operations to the Canary Islands' branches during the period of the war. Some of these funds were utilised by Artus to acquire the Dehesa Baja and Orovales farms. These purchases had the immediate effect of generating much local employment, both in their conversion to efficient banana plantations and, in the case of Orovales, in the construction of an irrigation tank of considerable capacity.

In contrast to precedent, on the specific instructions of Richard, Frank Artus was directed to purchase another and larger farm, La Costa. In the context of the general expansion of the Firm, this may sound like an innocent but routine transaction. Certainly it fitted into the general policy and the farm soon became one of the principal banana plantations owned and operated by the Firm for the next half-century. But there was more to it than appears from a quick reading of that first statement; a series of apparently-unrelated events need to be reassembled in order to gain an understanding of the whole.

The son of the Spanish vendor of La Costa had studied medicine in Madrid before going on to practise in Germany, hence he spoke German and had connections there. In later years he gave up practising medicine and went into politics, becoming the Mayor of Puerto de la Cruz for more than a quarter of a century, spanning the period at the start of the major tourist development in the 1950s/1960s.

Two years prior to the outbreak of the Great War, the principal hotel, the Taoro, had been taken over by German management and had become very popular with the few German residents who then lived within the Orotava Valley. Situated on the high promontory immediately behind the village of Puerto Orotava, the hotel enjoyed unobstructed views over all the valley as well as to Mount Teide and out over the sea.

In 1912 a sanatorium and, nearby, a meteorological observatory were constructed in the Cañadas, at the foot of Mount Teide at an altitude of about 7,500 feet. The scientific instruments were provided by the Kaiser Wilhelm Gesellschaft, an agency created just three years prior to the outbreak of the Great War for the purpose of providing the German Government with the means of establishing scientific research projects in those parts of the world which "fell within the scope of Germany's foreign policy". The "sanatorium" never housed any patients. In later years the "meteorological observatory" was dismantled and moved to a different site, not very far away but very much more suitable than the site originally chosen for the proclaimed purpose.

Also in 1912 the Prussian Academy of Science chose the island of Tenerife to establish an anthropoid ape research station to conduct experiments regarding the ability of apes to reason and to solve problems like humans. For this purpose they leased a large rural property situated on a headland half a mile out of the village of Puerto Orotava – a beautiful situation enjoying an unobstructed view both over the sea and towards the mountains. Since there were no native apes in Tenerife, however, it was necessary to import the animals from the Cameroons, part of German equatorial Africa from the latter part of the previous century until the Great War. The animals were landed at the little port of Puerto Orotava in December 1913, just a few weeks before Herr Doktor Wolfgang Köhler arrived with his wife and children to supervise the research station. He and his family lived in the station for the next three years and neither he nor any of the family ventured out of the compound "because he was afraid of the British". The apes themselves were kept in large cages and the experiments could have equally been carried out in any zoo in Germany, if the inconvenience of distance to the German colony of Cameroon had been an important consideration. Indeed, the choice of Tenerife seems curious as it certainly does not offer any of the natural advantages which either Cameroon or Germany itself would offer. Furthermore, although the experiments were duly carried out and documented, within some six months they were complete. But it was not until 1920 that Dr Köhler hurriedly departed from Tenerife.

It would be the best part of half a century before the island enjoyed a reliable and universal supply of electricity but in those primitive days not only the Taoro Hotel but also the two "scientific research stations" each had their own electric generators.

When war broke out in 1914 and the few tourists who had been coming to the island could no longer do so, the Taoro was closed as a hotel. However, it was still occupied by those of the German staff who were living there.

Spain remained neutral during the Great War but the sympathies of much of the population were towards Germany. While the war was fought principally within the continent of Europe, nevertheless the Atlantic was an increasingly important area of naval warfare. One of the principal problems in controlling a naval fleet was that of communication, radio being still relatively primitive but the only system available. Naval surface warships, fuelled by coal-burning engines, depended to a great extent upon speed and their steam boilers consumed enormous quantities of coal when steaming at full speed. Thus they were required to refuel after barely one week, so that the ready availability of supplies was an important factor in supporting an effective naval fleet. For the first time in a major conflict they were supported by the new submarines. Primitive by modern standards, they were powered by diesel when surfaced and electricity when submerged, with the batteries requiring frequent recharging on the surface. All of this meant that the submarine's effectiveness, like that of the surface warship, depended to a very great extent on the ready availability of fuel supplies. Despite this limitation, however, German U-boats were credited with sinking some fifteen million tons of Allied shipping during the Great War.

Additionally, three of the groups of mid-Atlantic islands – Azores, Madeira and Cape Verde – belonged to Portugal, which was much more sympathetic to the Allies. All of these factors made the Canary Islands a zone of very special interest to the German authorities, both as a potential source of fuel supplies and of intelligence. Moreover, the complex logistical problems of naval warfare required close coordination and the accurate and reliable transmission of intelligence. The British set out in the earliest days of the war to impede Germany's Atlantic radio communication network.

British Foreign Office files and German military records indicate a great deal of diplomatic activity, from the very first days of the war, regarding espionage activities of the Germans in the Islands. Information regarding shipping movements (such as the communiqué to the German Naval Staff on 19 October 1916 regarding the "armed British Yeoward Line steamer *Alondra*") was reported not only in the principal ports of Las Palmas and Santa Cruz, but also in other parts of the Islands. Diplomatic efforts to encourage the Spanish authorities to honour their neutrality and to impede military-related activity by Germany were conspicuously less than successful. Short of direct aggressive intervention, there was not much that could be done, other than to rely on indirect measures concentrated directly upon the local German activities themselves.

The Taoro hotel, closed to the public during the war, was in fact the local centre for espionage activities. The mountain "meteorological station" was first and foremost a major element in the German Atlantic radio network. The "ape research station" on the nearby beautiful clifftop was in fact the La Costa farm and was primarily a base for direct contact with the extensive

U-boat fleet working in that part of the Atlantic. Many of the vessels were frequently observed sailing close to the cliffs at night, where they would be able to pick up low-powered radio signals which would be too weak to be detected further offshore. All three of these establishments were set up a mere two years prior to the outbreak of war and all three were equipped with electricity generators, essential for radio communication.

When "Casa Yeoward" took possession, Herr Köhler and his "ape research station" were forced to move from La Costa to a site situated further inland, out of range of radio contact with the U-boats.

To support his instruction to Frank Artus to purchase the La Costa farm, Richard Yeoward transferred sterling, exchanged at 15 pesetas/£1, to Tenerife. This was also used to finance the considerable amount of work required as Yeoward proceeded to develop the banana production on the farm in accordance with its own standards. This gave employment to eighty families at a time when no other work was available and it represented a very important investment in the local economy.

Having tasted the bitterness of direct losses and suffered its share of tragedy, the partnership which had created the business less than a quarter of a century beforehand was destined to suffer its gravest blow. On 10 April 1916 the younger brother in the partnership, Lewis Yeoward, died at the age of forty-eight at his home at Mayfield, Ledsham, Cheshire, from paratyphoid fever, having been ill for forty-eight days. He left a widow and two teenage children and had nominated as Trustees of his estate his widow Ida Evans Yeoward and his brother Richard. As an initial measure to enable the business to be administered in the Canary Islands, the Trustees granted a power of attorney to Frank Artus, so that he could act for the estate "throughout the Canary Islands" and not only in Orotava where he was the manager. Regardless of the date Artus actually joined "Casa Yeoward" in comparison to both Fisher in Las Palmas and Smith in Santa Cruz, he had undoubtedly become the senior member of the Canary Islands team during the critical years of the business development.

chapter three

1916–1939

LEWIS Yeoward's death cannot have been a surprise to his brother Richard. He had been ill for a long time and the outcome can hardly have been in doubt in the days when mortality was a much more frequent visitor even for the most minor of illnesses. It left Richard, however, alone in charge of a sprawling business, at an age – he was now fifty-one – when he could perhaps have expected fewer responsibilities. Richard had two sons but Raymond, his eldest child, had joined the Firm only the previous year at the age of eighteen, while Bernard, the youngest, was still only twelve. Lewis had left one son, Cyril, who was only fourteen when his father died and still had no real idea whether or not he wished to participate in the business. Until he was old enough to make that decision, a place had to be left open for him. In due course Cyril was taken into the business by his Uncle Richard and, having worked there for a short time, quickly decided that he had no interest in pursuing a long-term career in the Firm. Once the decision had been taken, he, together with his mother and sister, further decided to sell Lewis's participation to Richard, thus taking their half of the partnership capital out of the business. Richard Yeoward therefore found that not only the entire burden of responsibility for the Firm was falling onto his shoulders but simultaneously he was being stripped of half of its net assets. Someone without Richard's character and determination might have reacted differently but he accepted the terms of the sale and the added operational responsibilities in an honourable manner. It was one of the many occasions when the family motto *Persevera per Severa* (Persevere through Difficulties) was upheld. The formalities of sale of the half-share were completed in 1922 and despite the change of legal status from a partnership to a sole proprietorship, the name of the business in England remained unchanged as "Yeoward Brothers", although in the Canary Islands it was changed to "Richard J. Yeoward". Two years later Raymond was admitted as a partner in the business, at the age of twenty-eight after working in the Firm for nine years.

In the meantime, Richard had other things to worry about. Lewis's death had come at a critical time. Yeoward had lost the guiding light behind its fruit business and one can only guess the effect as a whole since records for the Liverpool business for the next quarter century have not survived. The records of the London branch, however, show that it made losses approaching £3,000 during the two years 1917 to 1918. It seems reasonable to assume, therefore, that this period was a similarly gloomy one for the rest of the Firm's United Kingdom fruit business.

Moreover, the burden faced by Richard increased when the growing threat to shipping from German U-boats led to the introduction of the convoy system and to a general requisition of shipping in 1917. It was the liner companies which had suffered the bulk of the requisitioning until then, since their vessels were regularly in British ports when the Government required a ship, while other shipowners sought to avoid such a fate by keeping their vessels out of British ports.

Following the loss of the *Avetoro*, the Yeoward Line had bought as her replacement the *Valdes* in 1916. She was quite a new ship, built just before the outbreak of war in 1914, and was renamed the *Avetoro*. She was a cargo ship, without any of the expensive fittings and accommodation to be found on the traditional Yeoward passenger liners, and on one occasion six of her crewmen were so drunk and incapable of work that the vessel had to be brought to an anchor overnight upon entering the Mersey from the Manchester Ship Canal. But the former *Valdes* was not even in service with the Yeoward Line long enough for her new name to be officially registered. On 17 February 1917, having been requisitioned and while on a voyage carrying fodder for the horses serving with the army in France, she followed the fate of her predecessor when she was torpedoed seven miles from Portland Bill by a torpedo fired from a submarine without warning. Chief Engineer Spence was killed outright in the engine room by the explosion and she sank with the loss of eleven lives.

Only two months previously the *Alondra*, on voyage from Liverpool to Las Palmas, ran aground on rocks off the south-east coast of Ireland. She was under the command of Capt. Taylor, who had evidently been depending on the Fastnet Light and had overlooked the fact that it was extinguished for wartime reasons of security. The ship was a total loss, although fortunately the crew were saved. As might have been expected, Capt. Taylor was invited to hand in his resignation from the Firm.

Yet another shipping loss was to follow, two months after the sinking of the second *Avetoro*, when the *Avocet* – the original vessel of the Yeoward Line – finally ran out of luck, even though she was now armed for defensive purposes with a single small gun. On 19 April 1917, north west of Fastnet, she was captured and sunk by a submarine, although all aboard her were rescued. The luck of the Yeoward Line had not completely disappeared, however, for if the worst had happened, the Line would have ended the war with only a single ship. As it was, there were two fortunate occurrences. On 14 August 1917 the *Ardeola* was west of Ireland when a submarine fired a torpedo at her and missed; less than a month later, on 13 September, the *Andorinha* was sailing south of the Irish coast when a torpedo from a submarine actually hit her but failed to explode.

With some of his staff having faithfully served the Firm for twenty years or more, Richard Yeoward, a very moral and very caring man, had become increasingly concerned about what their future financial security would be when the time eventually came for them to retire. This future now took on a new urgency, as ships were being sunk by enemy action causing the loss of life of some of his crew and the consequent financial hardship for their families. Richard's brother-in-law was at that time the senior accountant for one of the country's largest shipping companies, so he discussed the problem with him. The outcome was the creation of the Yeoward Superannuation Fund, for which Richard created a Trust Deed and provided a personal donation of eleven thousand pounds sterling. The rules provided in this Trust Deed were far-reaching, even including the futuristic possibility of contributions and benefits being related to annual salaries as high as five hundred pounds (the salary of the highest paid executive was then £250 p.a.). At that time only the very large banks, insurance and shipping companies had such pension funds for their staff and the Yeoward Fund must have been one of the very first to have been created by a family firm – a generous and far-sighted advance in social welfare.

The second s.s. Aguila – c.1930.

As it was, the Yeoward Line ended the war with three vessels, of which the *Andorinha* and the *Ardeola* were only seven and six years old respectively, while the Line's youngest steamer was the second *Aguila*. She had been delivered in November 1917, more than three years after she had been ordered, during which time her costs had risen by a further 8%, quite a modest increase in inflationary times, to a total of £68,500. The second Yeoward liner over 3,000 tons, she could accommodate eighty-two passengers in comfort with the capacity for a further thirty-nine if required and she boasted more than 129,000 cubic feet of cargo space. An elegant vessel, she was regarded as being somewhat haughty and austere. On one of her first voyages, in August 1918, she successfully rescued the entire crew of the Scottish cargo vessel *Girasol*, which had sunk suddenly in the Irish Sea.

Towards the end of the war the Firm was appointed as temporary manager for a number of other vessels, including the Norwegian ships *Mirjam* and *Drammenseren* (captured while laying mines), the *Balmore* of John Holt & Co., the Danish *Belgien* carrying fruit from Spain and the fruit carrier *Petridge*.

After the war was over, Richard was determined to modernize and rebuild his shipping fleet which had been so devastated and at the same time to take advantage of the opportunity to reorganise the legal framework of the Yeoward Line. Previously, each vessel had been owned by a separate company (e.g. Aguila Steamship Co. Ltd.) "incorporated with the objects among other things of purchasing or acquiring and working a steamship called the *Aguila* together with all the requisite equipment for the same and to build, purchase or otherwise acquire any other steamship or shares therein but so that the company should not at any time own more than one steamship".

Now in February 1920 all were brought together in the one company, Yeoward Line Ltd., with a registered capital of one million pounds and as a result all the individual companies were put into voluntary liquidation. The objective of Yeoward Line Ltd. was to "purchase or otherwise acquire, and to undertake all or any part of the business, property, assets and liabilities of the following Companies, namely: … [the Memorandum listed six Steamship Companies under the management of Yeoward Brothers] … To purchase or otherwise acquire the steamships *Aguila*, *Andorinha*, *Ardeola* and any other vessels and, in particular, vessels under the management or control of the Firm of Yeoward Brothers."

This made no difference, however, to the practical operations – the new company simply owned the vessels and employed the Firm of Yeoward Brothers to manage and operate them. Richard, by this time, had quite clearly decided that his business was sound and the idea of limiting his responsibility behind separate limited-liability companies was not for him. It is interesting to note that, although not yet a partner, this is the first recorded occasion when Richard's eldest son Raymond was a signatory to such a document.

While the values placed upon the surviving three ships were possibly inflated because of the high values prevailing immediately after the war (at £390,000 this was nearly two-and-a-half times the price paid for them), of more interest was the value of the remaining assets held within each company. The three operating companies held cash in excess of £160,000. This was more than doubled by the inclusion of the other companies whose vessels had been lost during the war and where the value of those vessels had been replaced by the insurance compensation payments. There was therefore no doubt that the Yeoward Line could afford to purchase further new ships.

1916–1939

Richard placed an order for two new steamers, of 3,445 tons, with the Caledon yard in December 1920. The first vessel, the *Alondra*, was delivered late in the following year but it was not until the end of 1922 that her sister ship, the *Avoceta*, was received by the Yeoward Line.

These two ships followed the pattern set by the *Aguila*, as indeed did the final ship ordered from Caledon, the *Alca* in 1927. They were all of a similar size, with the largest, the *Alca*, being only 500 tons larger than the *Aguila*. All these vessels were built with the distinctive three-masted Yeoward profile and while the style of the Yeoward Liners was now considered to be rather conservative, Richard saw no need to change just for the sake of change. The modern motorship was not adopted by British shipowners with any enthusiasm after

s.s. Alca anchored off Madeira in the late 1930s.

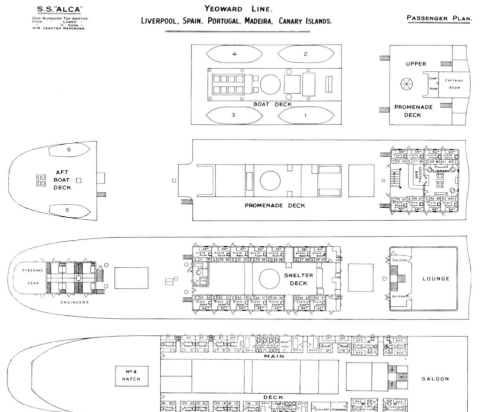

Passenger Plan – s.s. Alca c.1935.

the war, despite its advantages, and the Yeoward Line never erred from its unwavering faith in the steamer. Triple-expansion engines with three coal-fired boilers powered all four vessels giving a top speed of 13 knots. They all had the large two-decked passenger house amidships, while the deck-house over the stern housed the crew. The four cargo hatches were worked by derricks from the masts and by steam winches. The passenger accommodation in all the ships followed the pattern adopted by the *Aguila* where all the cabins were outside ones, with their own portholes or sliding windows and many with electric fans. Those on the promenade and bridge decks had access directly onto deck. "Each steamer also has handsomely decorated and artistically furnished Cabins de Luxe, each accommodating two passengers" and "All berths are fitted with 'Nesta' spring mattresses", said the Yeoward Line's "General Passenger Information" brochure, going on to indicate "wireless telegraphy for transmission of passengers' messages through ship or shore stations as they pass" – a clear reminder of the still-limited range of communication between the wars. There were four public rooms. The dining room lay on the shelter deck beneath the fore end of the superstructure, with a smoke room and bar on the port side and a drawing room on the starboard side above. A library and writing room with fitted desks was situated at the fore end of the promenade deck. Indeed, the ships were very well-endowed with public space. Another aspect to which great attention was paid was the improved provision of fresh food for the passengers and this led to the installation on all ships of a device nicknamed the "Iron Cow". This was a machine which provided fresh "milk" – a genuine novelty at sea at that period and it also gave rise to great curiosity.

Typical interior views of a Yeoward Line steamer in the 1930s.
Top: Cabin de Luxe.
Bottom: Main Deck Stateroom.

When the *Alondra* first appeared on the Canary route in 1922, the Yeoward Line was able to increase its fortnightly service to a weekly one. This enabled even more of the popular Yeoward cruises to be offered and at the peak of their popularity the Line operated six steamers after the introduction of the *Alca* in 1927. Berthed for the first time at the Firm's appropriated berth at Coburg Dock in Liverpool and while preparing for her maiden voyage, two potential passengers arrived early one morning, asking for the purser who was to show them over the vessel. At that moment the purser had not arrived but Richard Yeoward, without introducing himself, offered to show them around. At the end of the visit the couple expressed their thanks for his

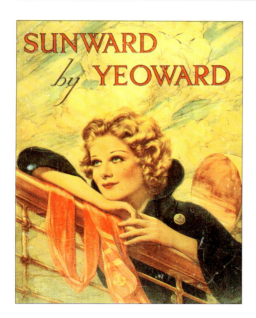
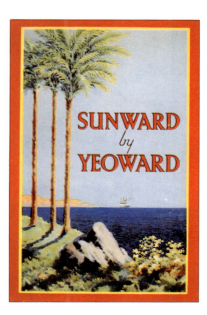

Far Left: Poster for Yeoward cruises with illustration modelled on Jean Harlow – c.1930.

Left: Cover of Yeoward Line brochure – 1931.

Below: Yeoward Liner "Aguila" in the River Mersey, outward bound for the Canary Islands in the 1930's, from an original painting by T. H. Shuttleworth.

Above: The Grant of Arms to Richard Yeoward, 1930, showing family motto "Persevera per Severa".

Right: View from the Yeoward offices in Puerto Orotava c.1930 showing one of the Yeoward Line steamers at anchor with passenger and cargo launches waiting to ferry the crates of bananas stacked along the quay. The previous Yeoward Line offices are shown on the right.

The second s.s. Alondra off Liverpool, passing the Liver Building – c.1935.

attention and handed him a tip of one gold sovereign, which he gratefully accepted. Later that morning in the office, the receipt of the first pound sterling earned by the *Alca* was duly noted in the Firm's accounts.

Cruises varied in length. In the summer of 1933, for example, the shortest cruise was one of eleven days costing from twelve guineas via Santander, Lisbon and Coruña, while the longest lasted twenty-two days from a cost of twenty-four guineas on a route taking in Coruña, Lisbon, Casablanca, Madeira, Las Palmas, sometimes Santa Cruz de la Palma, Puerto Orotava, Santa Cruz de Tenerife and a return visit to Las Palmas before heading back to Liverpool. The Line offered not only its round-cruise tickets but also return tickets for specific ports and special return tourist tickets, which allowed a break of journey at any port. The latter two ticket versions permitted the holder to complete the journey at any time within a period of twelve months. At that time British passengers were still being advised that it was not necessary for them to carry passports on their journey.

s.s. Ardeola and s.s. Avoceta in Madeira – early 1930s.

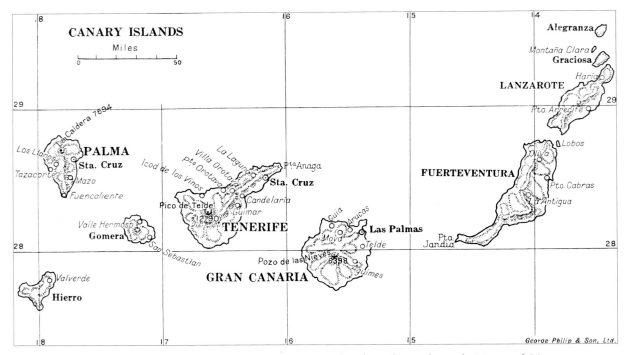

Canary Islands map in early 1930s.

The *Avoceta* was reputed to have been the only Yeoward Line steamer to have visited Puerto de la Cruz during the winter, when the off-shore anchorage was normally considered unsafe due to the seasonal unpredictability of sea conditions. This unusual visit occurred one year on 24 December, in glorious summer-like weather with a calm sea and not a cloud in the sky. The vessel appeared early in the morning after being ordered by radio to divert from its normal destination of Santa Cruz de Tenerife and, as a precaution, the pilot anchored it in the outer anchorage. When there is such good weather at that time of the year, the tidal currents are off-shore, causing the vessel lying at anchor to lie with its bow heading towards the shore – the position which the *Avoceta* quickly adopted. She was an impressive sight, the only vessel in the area and bathed in the glorious winter sunshine. An excursion was improvised for the eighty cruise passengers and they were sorry to have to return to the ship at midday for the passage round the coast to Santa Cruz. Once under way, however, they were amply compensated when Capt. Pope took them through the narrows inside the Anaga Rocks off the north-east corner of the Island, a sight which inspired many expressions of wonder and appreciation, as the ship's siren echoed off the cliffs giving the impression that the ship was being bombarded simultaneously from several positions along the coastline. Thus the *Avoceta* arrived in Santa Cruz in good time for the passengers to attend the gala fiesta which the Nautical Club had arranged for them to celebrate Christmas Eve. Why the unusual diversion of the vessel? While it is quite true that the passengers were absolutely delighted with the unexpected extra bonus, to understand the true reason requires an understanding of the inner workings of certain parts of the Firm. In those days, communication by land was poor and the only "cargo" destined for Puerto de la Cruz was the Christmas turkeys and presents sent from Head Office to the expatriate British staff! If the vessel had gone direct to Santa Cruz, the turkeys would have arrived late for the British Christmas dinners! This incident caused incredulous hilarity amongst the local staff (for whom there were no turkeys, this being considered at that time an essentially British custom) but it clearly demonstrates the attitude of relative autonomy which had developed in the Islands over many years. Several decades later, one of those staff, by then retired, was to write: "The new Yeoward generation do not discriminate. The previous ones neither, as we have since discovered from subsequent experiences – it was only the English managers who represented the Yeoward interests in the Canaries who discriminated."

Equally, it was the captains of the Yeoward Line who were largely responsible for the character of the vessels they commanded and which proved so attractive to countless numbers of passengers. In the main these masters were excellent seamen although a number of them met their downfall either through an addiction to the bottle or a passion for the ladies. In this latter category, Capt. Hugh MacLean managed to retain his job despite running his ship aground near Rhosneigr in the Isle of Anglesey, where Richard Yeoward had his country home, but Richard never tolerated lax morals in any of his staff and when MacLean's marital infidelities proved too much for his wife, who left him, he was dismissed even though he was then a senior captain in the Line. Another captain, Thomas Clatworthy, suffered a similar fate when he was compelled to leave the Line after an episode involving a married lady passenger.

There were, however, many fine captains who did not suffer such mishaps. William Welsh had been captain of the *Avocet*, the original ship of the Line, until in 1909 he was promoted to Marine Superintendent, the position he held until his death in 1938.

George Pope, who was appointed the master of the *Andorinha* in 1922, had trained under sail and was reputed to be a hard taskmaster. Very able and well-respected by those under him, he was a sociable, jovial character, who died in service. Leslie Scott, a perfect gentleman, if something of an authoritarian, had been in command of the second *Avetoro* when she had been sunk. His weakness was his special liking for the bar of the British Club in Tenerife. He was promoted to Marine Superintendent when Capt. Welsh died but did not adapt well to the land-based job and retired at the outbreak of war in 1939, to be replaced by Donald McPhee.

McPhee was a strict Sabbatarian, who neither smoked nor drank. Crew members wishing to be retained by him for the next voyage of his ship were expected to attend the Sunday morning shipboard service with regularity. He even attempted to close the ship's bar on Sundays but was mildly reprimanded by Capt. Welsh when a number of passengers complained. A steadfast character and a great mariner, he had trained on sailing ships. Promoted to captain in 1922, he once brought the *Aguila* into Madeira and Las Palmas under auxiliary steering power since she had fractured her rudder, for which prowess Lloyds awarded him their Silver Medal and the sum of £200. Such deeds no doubt contributed to his being pardoned after grounding the ship in fog on the Faraloes reefs, north of Lisbon – that and the fact that he successfully refloated the vessel without need of external assistance.

John Prendergast became the senior captain of the Line in the 1920s. He commanded the new *Alondra* in 1922 and likewise the maiden voyage of the *Alca* in November 1927. Harold Martin was the first Yeoward Line captain not to have trained under sail. He was a prudent seaman, serving principally as relieving master and having command of all of the vessels on different occasions. He was in command of the Yeoward liner which arrived in Tenerife on the morning of 18 July 1936, coinciding with the outbreak of the Spanish Civil War, and of the *Avoceta* when she was torpedoed in 1941. He was subsequently saved after being washed off the bridge as she sank. Arthur Frith was an able and keen-sighted seaman, whose qualities were not found wanting during his long service with the Line, especially in the Second World War. George Affleck, a corpulent man and an excellent seaman whose presence inspired confidence, began his service with the Line on the *Avocet* in 1908 and he commanded the *Ardeola* during the Second World War, surviving capture. Alfred Jones, who joined the Line in 1915, made his reputation as third officer of the *Ardeola* both as an athlete and as the officer best able to control a rough band of young apprentices.

The chief engineers were also an essential complement to the ship's masters and they too were apparently a class apart. Compared with the deck officers, the senior engineers were a most sober, steadfast and demure body. Among this upright group of men, the most notable included David Andrew, the senior chief engineer during the 1920s, a small, teetotal Scot. Arthur Lumley, a bombastic extrovert of a man, who was teetotal but loved to smoke his pipe, was often unpopular with the crew for failing to get his ship home in time, his priority being fuel economy.

On cruise ships, as the Yeoward liners were, the stewards and stewardesses were also important members of the crew. There were bath stewards, boots stewards, bar stewards, in fact there were stewards allocated to attend to almost every need a passenger had. One of the most successful chief stewards on the Line was H. E. Waugh. To supplement his earnings, he pocketed fees received from passengers for providing them with any better accommodation which might have been available. Others often kept the fares for inter-island passages, took backhanders for purchasing supplies on the Islands or otherwise traded on their own account. Richard Yeoward was reported to have told one exposed offender "There's no room for two financiers in this Company – and I'm staying." Eventually Mr Waugh was appointed victualling superintendent, on shore, in which position he enjoyed Richard's total confidence.

Of the rest of the crews who served with the Yeoward Line much less is known. There were changes in a ship's crew with almost every voyage but the engagement of crews for the Yeoward Line steamers was never a problem. The regularity of service appealed to them, with the monthly turnaround enabling them to spend a week at home after each three-week voyage. As was usual for the day, every voyage had its share of occasional desertions and fines for disciplinary offences. The most frequent of the latter was drunkenness, often involving overnight absence without leave from the ship. One occasion in particular is worth noting: at half past ten one evening, while the *Alca* was berthed in Santa Cruz, Greaser Jones and Fireman Judge were returning to the ship after a more than enjoyable night on the town. Jones stumbled on the lower platform of the accommodation ladder. Judge tried to save him but in doing so both men fell into the water between the ship and the quay. It fell to sixty-two-year-old seaman James Quinn, who was on gangway duty at the time, to go in after them and keep them both afloat while lifelines were attached to them and they were hauled aboard again. None of them appeared any the worse for the incident but only three months later Quinn collapsed and died on board the same vessel. He was buried in the Roman Catholic cemetery in Tenerife.

There were also occasional deaths on board ship, both of members of the crew and of passengers. Every Yeoward vessel carried a ship's doctor and occasionally, when he could not cope, crewmen who fell ill had to be left in hospital in the Islands or in Lisbon and collected on a later voyage when they had recovered. A recurrent seaman's complaint was venereal disease, typical of which was that suffered by the galley boy aboard the *Aguila* in 1939 – "Treatment: isolation, clap mixtures, light duties", recorded the ship's log book. Sometimes a passenger fell overboard. Captain McPhee was involved in two such incidents. In November 1932 one passenger, a farmer from Nottinghamshire, was reported missing aboard the *Avoceta* when the steward taking him his early morning tea found that his bunk had not been slept in. He had last been seen in the early hours of the morning returning to his cabin after obtaining a stout from the nightwatchman. A search of the vessel found no trace of him and he was presumed drowned. The second incident had a happier ending and exhibited the qualities of seamanship for which so many Yeoward masters were renowned. When a passenger was reported to have fallen overboard, McPhee, instead of swinging round at once to pick up the passenger, calmly ordered a marker buoy to be dropped overboard and certain crew members to keep sight of it and not be distracted by anything else. Meanwhile, the helmsman was told he should steer a precisely straight course as immediately beforehand while speed was reduced. After a prudent distance another buoy was dropped and more crew ordered to keep it in sight, while the ship was turned and manoeuvred to face back along the precise alignment of the two bouys. Within minutes the ship hove to precisely alongside the passenger who had fallen overboard. He was rescued without fuss or harm, whereas if the ship had been swung round at once it would have been almost impossible to find such a tiny speck in a huge ocean.

So, every Saturday throughout this period, a Yeoward steamer moved from its cargo-loading berth at the North Coburg Dock out into the Mersey, where it either berthed at Princes Landing Stage to embark the passengers or lay at anchor in mid-stream while they were ferried out to her by tender. With every passenger aboard the cruise could begin, with the steamer proceeding down the Mersey, one ship among many, towards the open sea. Four days out to sea, according to Yeoward's cruise brochure from the 1930s, and the Barlenga Islands were sighted "like grey lions in the heat haze". Lisbon, the first port of call, was absurdly likened to Torquay by one lady passenger, "one of those travellers who are always finding resemblances abroad to places at home". A sightseeing tour around the city took in a Portuguese bullfight. At Madeira, before the passengers left on their excursion of the island, the steamer was surrounded in the early morning by several rowing boats full of young boys who implored the passengers in a mixture of Portuguese and sailor's English to throw pennies that the boys might dive for into the water. Thirty-six hours later and the ship berthed in Las Palmas where it might be imagined that the port's "chief industry is the sale of Spanish shawls and mantillas to steamer passengers". At the end of the day the steamer's siren beckoned passengers back to the ship after they had danced the night away at the Royal Nautical Club. In Tenerife there were plenty of opportunities for sightseeing, swimming and basking in the warm sunshine. Then, after a visit to Orotava where "the sun-drenched Valley of Orotava is far more like one's idea of Paradise than the rainy hills of Connemara", it was time to set out once again for the Mersey and Liverpool.

The days on board were long. They started when the cabin steward brought tea at seven in the morning and ended not before 10.30 p.m. when the smoking-room steward produced plates of sandwiches. Four meals a day were served, breakfast, luncheon, afternoon tea and finally dinner at 7 p.m. Things were perhaps a little more relaxed than they had been before the Great War, since, while evening dress for dinner was still "customary", it was also "quite optional". There was never a dull moment for those passengers who wanted a lively holiday. On every cruise "an active Sports Committee of fellow tourists" was soon formed which organised games of deck tennis, golf, billiards, quoits, bull board, peg quoits and shuffleboard. It was possible to take a dip in the "good-sized, open-air swimming-pool, amidships on the promenade deck, the water being warmed when necessary". There was a daily "sweep" to which each passenger made a small contribution for estimating to the nearest mile the number of miles covered by the ship from one day to the next. More peaceful relaxation could be had by sitting in the deck-chairs on "that quiet part of the promenade deck or upper bridge deck" and reading a book selected "from the abundance of the lighter sort of reading afforded by a well-stocked and

Lounge, s.s. Avoceta.

Menu signed by passengers (including Raymond Yeoward and his wife) and crew, from the farewell dinner at the end of the cruise. s.s. Avoceta – March 1935.

up-to-date library". The wireless was available to listen to and it provided music during mealtimes and for dancing. There was also a toilet saloon "in the charge of an experienced hairdresser". At the end of the cruise came Charity Night when an auction was held of packs of the ship's playing cards, signed menu cards and the official chart of the voyage, the proceeds going to various shipping charities. This was followed by the fancy dress ball held along the promenade deck, sprinkled with French chalk for dancing, beneath an awning hung with gaily coloured bunting.

On a Yeoward cruise, one excursion which most passengers usually enjoyed was a visit to "a typical banana plantation" in the Orotava Valley where they were given a picnic in a small wood. Although barely a couple of miles from Puerto Orotava, it represented a full-day excursion before the days of motor-coaches. In those days "Casa Yeoward" employed two men whose job it was "to tidy up the wood after the weekly visit of the tourists".

The Firm's offices in Puerto Orotava were situated at that time in a charming old building which Frank Artus had been able to purchase. It was built in the classical Canary architecture, on two floors with a superb large internal patio and a typical wooden balcony directly overlooking the little port. The growing presence and importance of "Casa Yeoward" was further illustrated when, during this period, the local Town Council decided to

The third s.s. Ardeola anchored off Puerto Orotava c.1925.

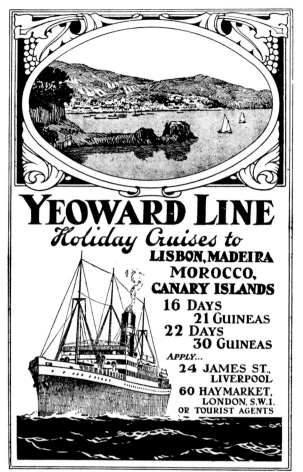

Early Yeoward Line poster as shown in the Canaries – c.1936.

accept the Yeoward tender to operate and take over the management of the port.

The maintenance of the farms in a good state of productivity during the war was to show handsome dividends for the effort invested. Inevitably, however, changes had to be made, partly due to Lewis's death but also because of local circumstances. The lifestyle which Frank Artus had led – whisky is a great companion but only in strict moderation – now meant that the time had come for him to take early retirement and he returned to England once he had left everything in perfect order. William Clark and Alfred Brabyn took over responsibility for farm management and for packhouse and shipping respectively.

Clark continued the Firm's policy of land acquisition with the purchase in 1920 of the San Antonio farm, situated between the British Club and the Anglican Church, followed later by the Dehesa and Lomo farms. Meanwhile, the Firm assembled a series of small landholdings which it grouped together to form the Llanos de Mendez farm and this became Yeoward's largest individual banana plantation. The transformation of the land into a farm gave work to approximately 300 labourers from dawn to dusk, six days a week, for several years. Soil was brought in ox-carts from forests higher up the Orotava valley and the work of creating terracing went on into the 1930s. The irrigation tank built in the farm, completed in 1928, was one of the largest on the island, holding nearly 100,000 tons of water. The weekly payment of wages usually lasted until about 10 p.m. on Saturdays.

The first lorries had appeared after the war and they created a problem for "Casa Yeoward" whose cart drivers, uneducated and neither able to read nor write, became redundant, while there was not a lorry driver to be found. As if by magic (but the type which only favours can produce), the cart drivers were provided with the necessary driving licences and overnight they became lorry drivers – learning to drive on the road could follow later. They were young and soon able to master the new technique, saying that it was "just the same as driving an animal, but faster". This development in turn led to the creation of the Firm's own garage-workshop. Spares were not available and whenever they were required it involved sending to Liverpool a drawing and description of the broken part, to eventually have a replacement shipped out.

Apart from the purchases of land, "Casa Yeoward" had also rented many properties which it developed into banana farms. These were leased for considerable periods of years, being initially either unplanted or in very poor state and were converted to productive farms by "Casa Yeoward". In many cases the owners were part of the local "landed class", who had inherited land but who lacked finance. Frequently the owner made it a condition of the lease that the Firm should employ one of their family. Sometimes this proved to be the least employable member and hence in years to come when the rental terminated, many well-known local family names were to be found amongst the staff. The largest of the rented farms were the thirty *fanegadas* of the two adjacent Gorborana farms. Others included the fifteen *fanegadas* of San Nicolas, ten *fanegadas* at La Galvana, adjacent to San Nicolas, eight *fanegadas* each at San Antonio Tolosa and La Carrera and there were various smaller farms. The twenty-five *fanegadas* at Los Principes were regarded as being of very poor quality for a banana farm. In 1930 "Casa Yeoward" acquired the French-owned business of Réné Piat, which brought another thirty rented *fanegadas* of bananas in Realejos, where most of the rented land was located.

William Clark's reluctance to forge a really close relationship with the local population has already been mentioned and the natural bridge between the British management and the Spanish population was the Secretary of "Casa Yeoward", Luis Herreros González, a native of Orotava. As the branch's senior Spanish employee, he was a very proud man, respected, even feared by some of the British members of staff. With a keen interest in politics, for which his mainly right-wing friends nicknamed him "the Bolshevik", he was a man of some influence and an invaluable assistant for Clark. When the latter was intending to visit Madrid to seek the resolution of some problem, he invited Luis Herreros to accompany him. In turn, Herreros considered such a major journey to the Spanish capital so significant that he arranged for his wife and daughters to accompany him. His disappointment, therefore, was enormous when, only hours before their departure, Clark received a cable informing him that the particular problem had been resolved and there was no need for him to visit Madrid. When Clark told Herreros, the latter could only clasp his head in his hands and exclaim "Oh, my God – what on earth can I do now, with the wife all dressed up, and the daughters bathed?" Sadly, Herreros died a young man in 1930.

At this time "Casa Yeoward" employed two general foremen, Amador and Bethencourt, one in the Realejos area and the other in the Orotava/Puerto de la Cruz area and they travelled around the farms under their supervision on horseback. The men were brothers-in-law, both from Gran Canaria and they were both regarded as a credit to the Firm. But then Amador bought himself a car, superior to that used by the manager, Mr Clark, whose view was that car ownership was not a privilege which belonged to the weekly paid and Amador was dismissed. Bethencourt managed to persuade the Firm to provide him with a car but this too rankled and it was not long before his job was also declared vacant.

By 1930 "Casa Yeoward" had become the largest banana grower in the Orotava Valley, producing some ten to twelve million pounds of fruit each year. Its operations covered about 100 *fanegadas* (130 acres) of rented farms and about 120 *fanegadas* (160 acres) of its own land, with extensive water rights attached to the land or owned independently.

The "water rights" are a story in themselves. The volcanic Canary Islands, off the centre of the Sahara Desert, have no surface water whatsoever: no rivers, no lakes, nothing. The annual rainfall, which varies considerably from region to region, averages about fifteen inches in the Orotava Valley but almost all of this falls in sharp tropical downpours during the winter months, leaving a period of six months with scarcely a drop of rain. Modern irrigation systems were unknown at that time and the only system available was to flood the ground from open channels every fortnight to the equivalent of two inches of rain in order to irrigate the banana plants with the large water intake they require. The problem might have seemed insoluble but thanks to private enterprise, combined with the ingenuity and hard work of the peasants, sufficient water was found. In Gran Canaria, and in later years in Tenerife, some wells were dug but they involved pumping up the water if found. In Tenerife most of the hills rise steeply and tunnels were perforated into the hillsides, slightly above the horizontal, so that if water was found it could flow by gravity. In the present day there are more than 1,500 miles of such tunnels, involving a truly enormous investment of capital and effort, all exclusively the result of private initiative and based on a law dating from the latter part of the nineteenth century which granted the ownership of any water found to the finder – and provided no subsidies to help. (This law has recently been replaced by one which takes away this ownership of the finder.) As a result, those persons who were interested formed themselves into private companies, agreeing to pay into the company a stipulated sum for each share in order to finance firstly the excavation and later, if water was found, its distribution. Either they would lose their entire investment if they failed to find or maintain water or they would have to continue making payments into

s.s. Aguila loading bananas at Santa Cruz in the 1920s.

the company so long as they held their shares. In return, they would receive a share of the water, measured by attributing a proportionate amount of "flow time" in each fortnight (to facilitate their irrigation sequence). From this basis a remarkably efficient free market developed in which some would use their own water, some would exchange it with others who had different sources of supply where this was mutually convenient to reduce loss by distance, some would sell their surplus and others would rent their shares on an annual basis. Thus the market was open to everyone and "water rights" joined land as the only two known investments until very recent times. To this day all municipal supplies in Tenerife depend upon this same source of water.

The principal banana packing-house, conveniently located on the sea-front near to the offices, had been rented for many years until it became possible to purchase it together with adjoining land. From there both the imported materials and the bananas packed for export could be directly ferried to or from the ships anchored off-shore. After it was purchased the old building was pulled down and a new custom-built packing-house of more than 3,600 square yards was built and inaugurated in 1927, with a great fiesta and dance. It was attended by not only the warehouse staff and their families but also by the farm and office staff – not to mention many others who just wanted to "join the party". More than 500 litres of Tacoronte wine and hundreds of cakes were consumed that night.

At this time, "Social Services"-type benefits were still totally unknown in the Canary Islands and therefore, as a key employee benefit, "Casa Yeoward" organised and funded a free medical pharmacy service for all their staff and families in each of the Firm's offices in Las Palmas, Santa Cruz and Puerto de la Cruz. In the Orotava Valley alone, staff numbered over 500 and the pharmacy service provided permanent part-time doctors in attendance. Until then infant mortality had been high but with the new service available the doctors were able discreetly to advise the young mothers (who otherwise would never have approached a doctor) about the need for hygiene for babies, giving them simple advice that, for example, their baby should be bathed at a certain hour each day. By this simple remedy of soap and water, which was quickly communicated amongst the local population, the mortality rate dropped significantly. In those days, when most houses had no running water installed, the importance of hygiene was not appreciated and this simple advice was destined to have a fundamental effect on the well-being of the population. In more serious cases, such as when one of the Firm's local stevedores suffered a broken leg or arm which could not properly be set locally, they were taken, at the Firm's expense, on the next ship to Liverpool for treatment there. Alas, human nature being what it is, the free pharmacy service was doomed to last only three or four years after abuses crept in, with staff - and friends - obtaining their prescriptions and free medicines which they then sold to others on the "open market".

Meanwhile, on the neighbouring island of Gran Canaria, the Firm had started to build up its own tomato farms. "Casa Yeoward" had for some time been involved in handling consignments of Canary tomatoes for the United Kingdom market. Most of the tomatoes grown in Gran Canaria, the centre of tomato-growing in the Islands, were shipped from Arinaga around the coast of the island to Las Palmas for transshipment onto calling steamers. In 1923, to facilitate this business, the Firm bought a warehouse immediately adjacent to the small wharf in Arinaga. In March 1924 Raymond Yeoward, just appointed a partner in Yeoward Brothers, sailed for the Canaries on the *Andorinha*. This was the first visit to the Islands made by a partner since Richard's last visit in 1912, although more recently the affairs of "Casa Yeoward" had come under the regular scrutiny of Joseph Wardle, the Firm's accountant, who visited the Islands for a month each year for a tour of inspection. On the occasion of Raymond's visit, the future of the Firm's operations in Gran Canaria were discussed and it was decided that "Casa Yeoward" should itself become involved in growing tomatoes. As a result, between 1925 and 1930, the Firm put together a farm for the cultivation of tomatoes in Sardina, near Arinaga. Following a strict policy of crop rotation, only some 30 of the farm's total of 204 *fanegadas* (some 280 acres –

surprisingly the local unit of land measurement, the "*fanegada*", is larger in Gran Canaria than in Tenerife!) were cultivated in any one year and the Firm's "Cock" brand of tomatoes enjoyed an excellent reputation for quality in Britain. Yeoward, however, remained only a medium-sized tomato-grower, there being several other holdings much larger than the single farm they possessed.

The development of the tomato business was the responsibility of the Las Palmas branch where there were quite frequent changes of management during this period. The original manager, Frederick Fisher, was compelled to leave the Island in 1930 and move to Barcelona. Although the law required an architect to be employed to supervise building work, this was largely ignored in many areas and Fisher followed local practice when he decided to have a warehouse built at Sardina. During its construction, three workmen were killed when part of the roof collapsed. Fisher was prosecuted for criminal negligence, forced to leave the Island and the Firm ordered to pay substantial compensation. Typically, Yeoward helped a loyal and long-serving employee by granting him an annual pension of £700, generous for the time, and thereafter sending consignments of tomatoes to his care. Prior to his leaving the Island, Fisher had taken his son Harry into employment in the branch. Harry was ambitious and when visiting Liverpool had sought an interview with Richard Yeoward at which he asserted that he, Harry, was worth £1,000 per annum. He received the curt reply: "Go and get it, don't let me stop you"; and this was the end of Harry Fisher's short career with the Firm.

Fisher was succeeded by Robert Humphreys who had been sent out to the Islands from the Liverpool accounts department shortly after the war but he succumbed to a heart condition only five years later and the post was then taken up by Victor Allen. He had been based in Puerto Orotava as the Firm's accountant and was more of an office administrator than a manager. He had little contact with the local community, this being left to his joint-manager Juan Perdomo.

The continuing increase in tomato-farming in Gran Canaria led to a rising demand for phosphates for land fertilisation. For a very short period from February to August 1928, the *Andorinha* extended her sailing itinerary to include Tangiers and Casablanca, bringing back phosphate to the Canaries and taking fruit homewards. This was short-lived for two reasons. Firstly the existing UK-Morocco shipping conference did as much as it could to snuff out what it saw as unwelcome competition and secondly the business was unremunerative anyway because of the already depressed state of the shipping market.

The poor state of the shipping market had an unwelcome effect upon the Yeoward Line. Only a year after the launch of the last and largest of the

1916–1939

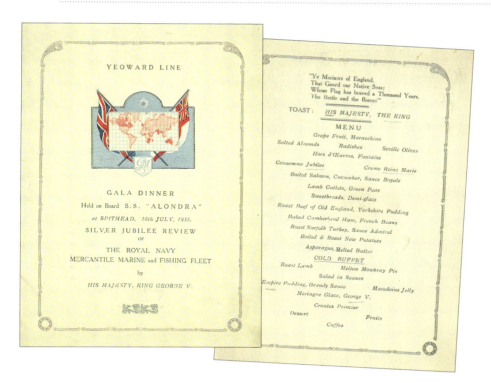

Menu for the Gala Dinner held on board the s.s. Alondra at the Silver Jubilee Review at Spithead, July 1935.

s.s. Avoceta off the Pier Head, Liverpool – c.1930. From an oil painting by G. Lawton.

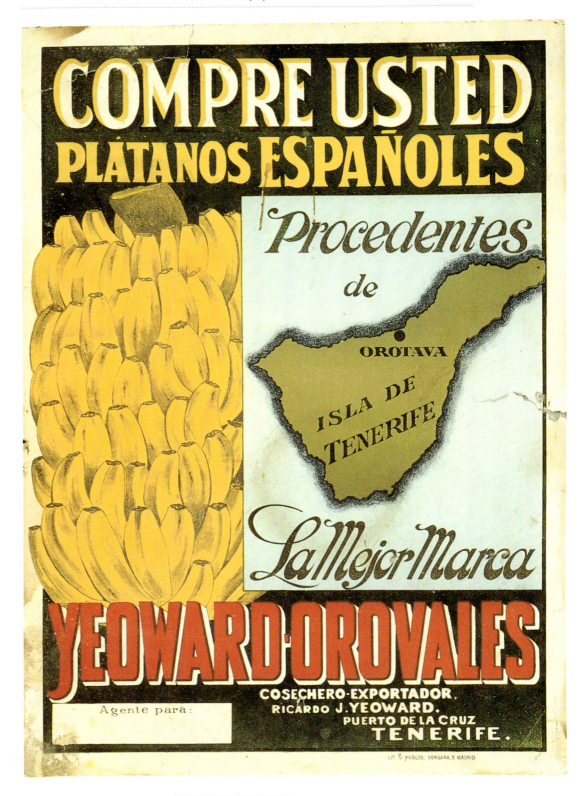

Poster as used on the Spanish mainland c.1929 promoting bananas from Casa Yeoward.

Yeoward steamers, the *Alca*, the failure of the phosphate venture led Richard and Raymond to agree to the mothballing of the *Andorinha* at the end of 1928 until her eventual sale in 1930 to Pacific Steam Navigation Co.

Having reached his sixty-fifth birthday, Richard Yeoward retired on 31 December 1929. In so doing he retained ownership of only a small holding of shares in Yeoward Line Ltd. and he planned that this, together with the real estate properties in the Canary Islands, would produce an income for his wife and himself during their lifetime. Thereafter it would be left to his three children in equal shares. All other assets without exception were considered to be assets of the partnership of Yeoward Brothers, including all its business activities in the Islands (and also the farming of the estates) wherever situated. On New Year's Day 1930 Raymond was joined in the partnership by both his younger brother Bernard Evans Yeoward and by Richard's most trusted assistant Joseph P. Wardle, until then the Firm's accountant. In this latter case, the appointment was for a specified period of ten years, at the end of which Joseph would retire on 31 December 1939.

Mr. Raymond Yeoward c.1930.

But in the case of Bernard Yeoward, the intention was that he would partner his brother for the remainder of their careers. This good intention was doomed to fail within the year. Bernard had many other interests in life and was unable to devote his attention adequately to the interests of the Firm and he subsequently resigned in October of that same year. He continued to participate in the shipping activities but only in his capacity as a Director of Yeoward Line Ltd. – which, it will be recalled, was merely the owner of the vessels, all aspects of their management and operation being contracted to the Yeoward Brothers partnership.

Thus it was that Raymond Yeoward and Joseph Wardle faced the very difficult economic circumstances of the recession of the 1930s and it is to their credit that the Firm survived to encounter better times some years later.

Now faced with the consequences of the recession, the Firm made great efforts to overcome the difficulties by adopting a very positive approach to the promotion of their cruises. Probably recalling the success of *A Letter Home*, their cruise brochure published in 1913, they published two new and attractive booklets in 1931: *In Search of the Sun – Yeoward Line*, the story of a typical cruise, and *Yeoward Line – Shore Excursions & General Passenger Information*. Trade on the Canary Islands route, however, declined during the depressed years of the 1930s and sometimes the steamers had to be gainfully employed in other trades to different parts of Europe and the Mediterranean, often, but not always, carrying passengers. Even this was not enough to keep the whole fleet in service and consequently the *Ardeola* was requisitioned in 1935 for duty as a naval stores base at Aden during the crisis attending the war waged by the Italians upon Abyssinia. Her passenger certificate was subsequently allowed to lapse. In 1938 the Chilean State Railway Company made an offer for the *Alondra* which the Yeoward Line could not refuse and the vessel was duly sold. In 1939 the remaining Yeoward vessels could be found as often elsewhere as on the traditional route to the Canaries. For example, in early 1939 the *Alca* sailed from Hull via Tilbury to Jaffa, Haifa and Algiers, before returning with her cargo of Palestinian fruit to Liverpool via London. During the summer of that year both the *Alca* and the *Avoceta* were sent on a number of Scandinavian cruises while the *Ardeola*, no longer with any passengers on board, was bringing back pyrites from Huelva.

Apart from the depressed state of the shipping market, exacerbated by the Civil War in Spain, there were other reasons why the steamers of the Yeoward Line were under-employed by 1939. The main reason was that the Yeoward Line steamers were increasingly old-fashioned. By the early 1930s Canary shippers wanted faster and more modern ships than the existing fleet of the Yeoward Line could provide. Attempts were made to meet these demands by making arrangements for the carriage of cargo from the Canaries with the Danish Torm Line and with MacAndrews but neither of these efforts was successful. In particular the arrangement with the Torm Line failed badly and threatened Yeoward's considerable reputation in the Islands as a result.

Why then had the Yeoward Line not placed orders for more modern, speedier vessels as required by the Canary exporters? This decision was the consequence of the contrasting attitudes taken towards the businesses as a whole by different members of the family. Richard Yeoward had retired at the end of 1929, gaining the distinction in 1932 of being appointed High Sheriff of Anglesey where he then lived. From his earlier holdings of more than 75% of the shares in Yeoward Line Ltd., he had retained only a small stake, transferring the remainder to his children Raymond, Evaline and Bernard. There were now, therefore, a number of family members who had no active interest in the business but who still retained shareholdings in the ship-owning company Yeoward Line Ltd. In addition to Bernard and Evaline, these included the family of the late Lewis Yeoward who had retained their investment in this company when they sold their interests in the remaining businesses to Richard.

The pressure from these members of the family for the realisation of their investments led to a reduction in the capital of Yeoward Line Ltd. in July 1933. This reduction was brought about by Lewis's family withdrawing their total investment of £150,000 and Bernard and Evaline reducing their investments by £100,000 and £27,000 respectively. These sums were paid partially in cash and the remainder by means of debentures which were to be paid off during the following ten years. In other words, in this way and at a time when the Yeoward business was beginning to come under some financial pressure, funds that could have been used to modernise the fleet were stripped from the Company.

Another reason for the under-utilisation of Yeoward vessels was the state of the Canary fruit trade, for by the end of the 1930s events outside the control of Yeoward had seen the almost entire disappearance of a market which had been extremely profitable less than a decade earlier. This was a double blow for the ships of the Yeoward Line because not only had homeward cargoes declined considerably but the carriage of outward cargoes to the Islands had also become largely unprofitable by this time.

Between 1930 and 1935, however, the Canary fruit trade remained very profitable for Yeoward. Britain had been the major market for fruit from the Islands for many years but by 1930 the Spanish mainland and European markets were also expanding rapidly and "Casa Yeoward" made the most of these opportunities. In 1930 the purchase of the business of Réné Piat in Tenerife had given the Firm an entry into the French market where bananas were sent principally to the Paris branch of the Spanish firm of Ballarin y Piera under the brand names of "Jolie" and "Maja". With no international telephone service yet available, communication had to be by telegram to their branch in Irun where their staff crossed the street (i.e. the international frontier!) and retransmitted by French telegraph from Irun to Paris. The business prospered until the Second World War. At the same time, Raymond Yeoward and Mr. Clark made a joint visit to Spain to appoint sales agents in

Mr. Richard Yeoward as High Sheriff of Anglesey, 1932.

Cadiz, Santander, San Sebastian and La Coruña, to exploit the mainland market to which Yeoward sent bananas under the brand name of "Orovales". This means "You are worth gold" and it was also the name of one of the Firm's banana farms in Orotava.

The continental market became even more important for "Casa Yeoward" because of an event which marked the beginning of the end for the Canary banana in the United Kingdom. In 1932 the Treaty of Montreal brought into being the Empire Preference system of import duties designed to discriminate in favour of the colonies of the British Empire. Canary bananas were compelled to carry the burden of an import duty of £2-10s-0d a ton, which became increasingly difficult to sustain in the face of competition not only from Jamaica and other Empire producers but also from cheaper fruit from South America.

In an attempt to bolster the marketing of the Canary bananas in England and thus endeavour to offset the declining exports to that market (and, of course, to boost the shipping cargoes at a time when they were in decline), Yeoward decided to establish a chain of retail fruit shops. Under the name of Cavendish Fruit Stores, ten shops were opened in the Birmingham area in towns such as Solihull and Leamington Spa. They were far enough away from the Firm's wholesale operations not to encroach upon the territory of existing customers and sited in an area with a population large enough to provide sufficient custom. Rather than employ an unknown fruiterer, it was decided to send a man of proven confidence to manage the shops. As there was then less justification for a victualling superintendent for the ships than had previously been the case, Mr. H. E. Waugh, the then encumbant, was transferred to the Cavendish job. Unfortunately, confidence sometimes fails and it came as a most unpleasant surprise to Raymond Yeoward some years later when he had to dismiss Mr. Waugh for theft.

At the same time as Cavendish Fruit Stores was being established, however, events in Spain were conspiring to undermine the purpose for which the shops had been opened. The Spanish monarchy was overthrown on 14 April 1931 and the proclamation of the Spanish Republic was accompanied by public rejoicing in the streets. Mr. Wardle arrived in Las Palmas that same day on a Yeoward ship from Liverpool, continuing to Puerto de la Cruz next morning. When Manuel Abreu went aboard, the chief steward asked him to go to Mr. Wardle's cabin. Later Abreu was to recount:

> *He asked what was likely to happen amongst the public, and naturally also about the working of the ship. I informed him in detail but he persisted with his questioning. I told him that all was calm, that the*

"fiesta" had been the previous day and that all was prepared for the unloading and loading without problems. The work was carried out without a hitch but Mr. Wardle, respectable and respected, with a reputation as an authoritarian and for firm and efficient decisions, that morning appeared to me faint-hearted and frightened and greatly reduced in stature.

The proclamation of the Republic brought with it a new national flag in the colours of red, yellow and purple. Since the foundation of the Yeoward Line, the House Flag had been and always remained the initials Y.B. on the horizontal central yellow band between red bands, i.e. similar to the original and subsequent Spanish national flag. Whenever one of the ships was anchored off Puerto de la Cruz, it had always been the custom to fly the House Flag from the mast over the Yeoward office overlooking the port. Early one morning, several months after the proclamation of the Republic, the officer in charge of the local Civil Guard (locally well-known for his monarchical beliefs) accompanied by two guards, presented himself in the Yeoward office, and ordered that the flag be lowered, "because the Spanish Flag is no longer the two-coloured one". Manuel Abreu was the person who received him, replying that "the flag which is flying has no national nor political significance. It is the House Flag of this Shipping Line". Being a local man, like Manuel Abreu, the officer knew this to be true but, believing he was carrying out his duty, he insisted Abreu carry out his instructions. The two men stood silent, each waiting for the other to make the next move until finally Manuel said "I am sorry that I cannot obey your orders. These will have to be referred to the Manager, who is still aboard the ship. However, if you have the necessary authority to make us lower the House Flag, I will permit you to go upstairs to the terrace so that you may lower it yourself." The officer, without another word, turned and left the office, accompanied by the two guards. The Flag remained flying until late that afternoon, when the ship raised anchor and sailed. Honour had been satisfied.

The early and middle 1930s was a very difficult period in Spain, with the prominence of the "Popular Front" eventually leading to the Civil War. For marketing bananas in the Spanish mainland, it was no longer feasible to remain totally independent. "Casa Yeoward" became a founder member of a new company in 1934 and, in line with political thinking of the day, this was given a name which would sound well in left-wing circles: "Sindical Exportabana S.A." One night during a period of revolutionary strikes in 1934, the Firm's warehouse in Orotava, holding large working stocks of packing materials (paper and straw) and chemical fertilizers, was set ablaze. The military authorities eventually brought the fire under control but only after heavy material losses. Furthermore, new legislation was being planned which would have obliged foreigners to sell any property in Spanish islands to Spaniards. Mr. Clark was obliged to spend many months in Madrid lobbying against the proposal until it was abandoned. The two largest banana growers in the Canaries at that time were Fyffes and Yeoward, both foreigners and faced with such unrest they reacted quite differently. "Casa Yeoward" ceased renewing farm rentals when the contracts expired and in other ways "battened down the hatches to weather the storm". In contrast, Fyffes sold up and departed. It would be very many years and a generation later before "Casa Yeoward" would be able to reap the benefits of their decision.

In 1936 the British Foreign Office and Embassy in Madrid had to become involved in the Firm's situation in the Islands, as a result of the social unrest and martial law. Immediate reinstatement of labourers dismissed for involvement in political strikes was demanded of "Casa Yeoward" by the authorities, without waiting for the implementation of normal legal procedures. These demands had to be accepted by Yeoward as the alternative was imprisonment for Clark and an embargo of the Firm's properties to pay indemnities to each farm labourer. In any case, if normal legal procedures had been followed and a court decision given which was unfavourable to Yeoward, there would have been no right of appeal. Eventually, the general unrest and uncertainty was resolved when the Military Governor of Tenerife, General Franco, was secretly flown by a private British pilot to take charge of the Spanish forces in Morocco, in preparation for a rising in the Spanish mainland. On 18 July the Civil War broke out.

Very early that morning the Yeoward ship, under the command of Capt. Martin, was anchored off Puerto de la Cruz, having come from La Palma. All was calm and normal in the village. The lorries loaded with bananas for Liverpool were waiting on the wharf and the cargo launches with their crews were waiting to start work. First the pilot went aboard, then the port health official and somewhat later, around six o'clock in the morning, Manuel Abreu arrived from the office. Immediately the captain called him and proceeded to tell him how they had sailed from La Palma without pilot, without documentation and at full speed. There the town was in a state of revolution with everyone in the streets, including soldiers who were shooting. Manuel listened in surprise, unable to comment and not having any other source of information at that early hour of the morning. The first officer gave the order to commence cargo operations. These were completed normally and the vessel was despatched for Santa Cruz that afternoon.

Meanwhile, when Manuel Abreu returned ashore about nine o'clock in the morning, the atmosphere was noticeably different. Although the labourers were worried, nothing unusual had happened but news had reached the office that a military *coup d'état* had taken place. At around ten o'clock they watched from the office window as an army unit, firing warning shots, arrived on the wharf and proclaimed military law. There had been few people in the streets but when the military unit appeared there were even fewer. The Town Council was dissolved and replaced by civilians carefully selected by the military authorities who were now in control. In the Canary Islands the coup had triumphed but in the Spanish mainland bloody civil war followed.

During the Civil War coinage almost disappeared, due mainly to the public hoarding it, and "Casa Yeoward" was forced to issue their own notes to pay weekly wages. These notes were always honoured in the local shops, with Yeoward exchanging currency for them upon demand from the shopowners. The Firm also set up kitchens again to provide free meals for those in need, although after a time it was compelled to do it under the aegis of the local Falangist Party, who found it unacceptable for a foreign firm to be dispensing such service but who were unable to continue the kitchens without "Casa Yeoward's" help.

With the Spanish economy thrown into chaos by the Civil War, however, it was not long before the mainland was only too grateful to receive supplies of domestically grown foodstuffs. The Spanish mainland therefore became more and more the main outlet for Canary bananas but this led to the formation of a state regulatory body for the marketing of the bananas. This was CREP (Regional Confederation for the Export of the Banana) and it was not enthusiastically received by the growers. In fact, the disruptive effect of the Civil War, State regulations and, finally, another World War meant that "Casa Yeoward's" fruit business became unprofitable from 1936 until at least 1943.

During the 1930s, therefore, Raymond Yeoward was faced with the consequences of both Imperial Preference and the Spanish Civil War. The former had resulted in falling demand for Canary bananas in Britain while the latter had reduced supplies to less than a trickle by 1939. In other words, more and more people in Britain no longer wanted to buy Canary bananas because they were too expensive, while those who did found fewer and fewer were available. This difficult situation was in contrast to the UK fruit trade in general which remained as bouyant in the 1930s as it had been for most of the 1920s. The growth, for example, in the importation of fruit from Palestine at this time provided alternative sources of income for Yeoward's fruit business. The London branch was dealing profitably for most of this period in American and Tasmanian apples, Brazilian and Spanish oranges, Egyptian potatoes and onions, as well as produce from Cyprus and British Columbia. Nevertheless, the Canary fruit charges and commission, accounting for almost 90% of its profits until 1938, had remained the most significant part of the Yeoward fruit business and in 1939 the contribution from this source vanished almost entirely.

The Firm's founder, Richard J. Yeoward, died peacefully in his sleep on 31 May 1937 at the age of seventy-two years. It was a beautiful early summer day and provides the earliest recorded memory for his grandson, Tony Yeoward. Tony, who was later to step into his grandfather's shoes, was then aged only four but he remembers that evening standing on the front doorstep of the family home at Caldy and turning to his mother, he pointed towards Birkenhead and asked "Mummy, is that Heaven over there?" One is left to imagine the innocent workings of a child's mind.

chapter four

1939–1945

AT the beginning of September 1939 the *Avoceta* was cruising in Norway and Sweden under Capt. McPhee. Suddenly the ship was ordered to cut short the cruise and return to Liverpool at full speed with all lights extinguished as war appeared to be imminent. The passengers were disembarked on the east coast of Scotland and returned to Liverpool overland while the ship sailed back to port around the north coast of Scotland. The *Aguila*, on the day that war was declared, 3 September 1939, was in Puerto de la Cruz. The darkness of the ship with all her lights out mirrored the mood of the passengers as the ship left port to make the potentially hazardous journey back home.

s.s. Aguila pictured here (c. 1939) at anchor in the River Mersey shortly before the outbreak of war.

At Head Office in Liverpool, staff were soon being called up for war service. This left Raymond Yeoward not only shouldering the whole of the responsibility for the direction of the business after the retirement of Joseph Wardle at the end of 1939, but with an increasingly ageing staff to assist him. This was the case with many firms during the war but it did not make life any easier. The situation was not helped when a number of the remaining staff were directed on secondment from 1941 onwards to the Bibby Line and the Coast Line. In May of that year Liverpool suffered heavily from German bombing which devastated large swathes of the city close to the river. Yeoward Brothers' offices in Harvey Buildings, together with most of its records, were completely destroyed by incendiary bombs on the night of 5 May. The quiet reserve which characterised Raymond Yeoward, now in his middle forties, was illustrated when he was confronted by the smouldering ruins of what had been elegant head offices only hours before. He merely remarked "Well, I don't think we'll get much done here today, we'd better get over to the Sale Room." Offices were re-established in much more spartan conditions above the premises of Yeoward's fruit saleroom at 33 to 35 Victoria Street.

Government control of shipping and food supplies, coupled with the increasingly heavy loss of merchant shipping through enemy action, brought about a rapid decline in imported produce. The Government actually banned banana imports from November 1940 but this made little difference to Yeoward because the supply of Canary bananas into the country had already dried up. The *Avoceta* was reputed to have been the last vessel to import Canary tomatoes into the United Kingdom during the war when she returned to Liverpool in April 1941. Certainly from the end of 1941 onwards there was little fruit business done at Liverpool, while the business of the London branch was confined to a limited volume of English produce which was insufficient to cover the branch's running costs. The losses incurred throughout the war at Liverpool and London were repeated at the branches in Glasgow and Hull (a branch opened between the wars), although the Newcastle branch contributed substantial profits to the Firm between 1942 and 1945. Yeoward Brothers as a whole, however, excluding the Yeoward Line and the business in the Canary Islands, made large losses between 1941 and 1943, before returning to profit, albeit a tiny one, in 1944.

In the Canary Islands, to reflect the changed situation brought about by the death of Richard Yeoward, the Firm now traded under the names of "Herederos de R. J. Yeoward" for the properties and "Raymond R. Yeoward" for the other business activities. The only wartime change of management occurred with the death of Alfred Brabyn in 1943 and his replacement as manager at Santa Cruz by William Shipley, whose greatest benefit to the Firm stemmed from his close ties with the local community. The fruit business, however, continued to lose money and in 1943 the Firm sold its six cargo lighters and two passenger ferries which had not been used since the outbreak of war. By now, the tentacles of state control had extended to the planting of crops. This did not affect the all-year-round cultivation of bananas but did affect the Yeoward tomato farm in Sardina where an order to plant tobacco was given by the authorities. Unfortunately, the authorities also declared that everyone, irrespective of the situation of the properties, should plant their tobacco at the same time. This meant that all the plants would be growing in June to October, precisely the most inappropriate season in Sardina. Representations to the authorities proved as useless as the resulting crop was destined to be.

The four steamers the Yeoward Line possessed on the outbreak of war, the *Ardeola*, the *Aguila*, the *Avoceta*, and the *Alca*, were soon all pressed into

The s.s. Alca dressed up for war off Iceland, 1943.

government service. A licensing system, to enable the British Government to secure the vessels it wanted, had been established upon the outbreak of war and a general system of requisitioning had been introduced in 1940. Between 1940 and 1942 all the Yeoward vessels were engaged at one time or another by the Government for the evacuation of British and allied refugees from Portugal, Spain and Gibraltar back to the United Kingdom. The *Alca* was withdrawn from this service at the end of 1940 and sent up to Iceland where she served for the rest of the war as a depot vessel.

As well as their official work of returning refugees to the United Kingdom, the ships also regularly brought back British and foreign seamen from various ports, where they had been landed after their own vessels had been sunk by the enemy, or they took on as crewmen foreign nationals stranded in neutral ports. In July 1940 for example, the *Avoceta* signed on nine Belgians and one Frenchman mainly as cabin boys and assistant stewards, although one acted as the ship's doctor and another as the ship's cook, for the return voyage from Lisbon to Liverpool. In July 1941 the same vessel at the same port engaged twenty Norwegians, three Latvians and one Dane as deckhands.

Both the *Alca* and the *Aguila* had had close encounters with the enemy during the summer of 1940 when the enemy U-boats were beginning to step up their attacks on allied shipping. In late May 1940 the *Alca* was sailing back to Liverpool from Las Palmas, carrying a cargo of bananas, forty crew and two passengers. She was armed for defensive purposes with a four-inch gun. At one o'clock in the morning of 28 May, the steamer was five days out from Las Palmas when a torpedo was fired at her and missed. Captain Martin ordered the ship to resume zigzagging which she had ceased upon the fall of darkness and the gun crew was put on action stations. An hour-and-a-half later the vessel was fired upon twice by a distant submarine, the first salvo falling short and the second passing overhead close to the mast. The *Alca* returned fire and the submarine broke off the engagement.

In another incident, the similarly armed *Aguila* sailed from Liverpool to Lisbon and Las Palmas on 7 August 1940 with 800 tons of general cargo, forty-two crew and one passenger. Twelve days later as the vessel was zigzagging at full speed between Lisbon and Las Palmas, she was attacked by gunfire from a submarine some three miles off her starboard quarter. In the heat haze on a flat calm sea the submarine was clearly visible. Within three minutes the *Aguila*'s gun crew had returned fire and the ship was steaming at a full fourteen-and-a-half knots on a zigzag course. For fifty minutes the submarine continued to engage the *Aguila* but the distance between the two was increasing all the time and some of the submarine's shots were beginning to fall short. The *Aguila*'s last half-a-dozen shots fell uncomfortably close to the U-boat which gave up the chase and the *Aguila* reached Las Palmas without further mishap.

Aguila in wartime paint at Las Palmas in 1940 after her successful gun duel with an enemy submarine.

A year later, on 13 August 1941, the *Aguila* set sail from Liverpool again but this time in convoy. She was armed with a four-inch gun, two Marlin guns and two PAC rockets. The convoy was bound for Gibraltar and hence was labelled OG (Outward Gibraltar) 71. The vessel's master remained Capt. Arthur Frith, a fair and fastidious man, respected and trusted and with a sense of humour. The *Aguila* was the largest vessel in the Liverpool section of the convoy, which met up with sections from the Clyde and from Milford Haven to form a convoy of twenty-two merchant vessels escorted by six naval corvettes, an ageing destroyer from the Royal Norwegian Navy and the sloop HMS *Leith*. The *Aguila* took pride of place as the convoy's commodore ship, the senior naval officer on this occasion being retired Vice-Admiral Patrick Parker. On board she carried seventy-seven crew and eighty-four naval personnel as passengers. These latter were mainly destined for Gibraltar and the Middle East. As well as the commodore, his five naval staff and five naval gunners, there was in particular a contingent of the Women's Royal Naval Service (WRNS) – nine chief Wren cypher officers and twelve other chief Wrens – and a naval nursing sister. Under longstanding Navy rules, women were not permitted to travel in warships and had to be found a passage upon an armed merchant ship in convoy. They were young women, most of them in their early twenties, although the youngest was only eighteen.

The convoy's course was abruptly changed shortly before it set sail. The new and shorter route took the convoy much closer to the western coast of Europe because many of the smaller merchant vessels were unable to carry with them the fuel needed for the original longer route, which would have taken the convoy away from the enemy's naval bases and out into the Atlantic. The first contact the convoy had with the enemy came on 17 August when it was shadowed for a time by a German bomber. The next day the convoy received its first warning from the Admiralty that U-boats were likely to be in the area. The ships safely endured a brief bombing raid by two German bombers but again received further warnings that several U-boats were active in the area.

This warning was borne out all too soon. At 1 a.m. on 19 August 1941 the escort destroyer, the *Bath*, was hit by two torpedoes and sank within three

s.s. Aguila, 1941, from a line drawing by Tom Shuttleworth.

Line drawing by Tom Shuttleworth depicting a Wren on board s.s. Aguila waving to an escort vessel – 1941.

minutes. Eighty-three of her complement of nearly 130 men were either drowned or killed by the depth-charges which exploded aboard the vessel as she sank. Ten minutes later the *Alva* from Glasgow was sunk, taking her 2,000 tons of coal to the bottom with her, but all her crew survived. As a result of this action, Capt. Frith had all his passengers standing by in life-jackets and the Wrens were instructed to remain together in the ship's library. At 3 a.m., however, there had been no further attacks and the passengers were allowed to return to their cabins to lie down but not to undress. Frith himself, after remaining on the bridge until a change of course had been accomplished, took the commodore's advice and went to take some rest upon the settee in the chartroom beneath the bridge.

At the very moment that the *Aguila*'s passengers were returning to their cabins, elsewhere in the convoy another merchantman, the *Ciscar*, was torpedoed twice and sank in forty-five seconds with the loss of thirteen lives. Ten minutes later, at 3.10 a.m. on that calm August morning, the *Aguila* was hit in quick succession on her port side by two torpedoes. The second torpedo extinguished all the lights on board the steamer and broke her in two. From the time the first torpedo struck the ship until she sank was less than two minutes.

When the first torpedo struck the ship, Frith later recalled that,

> *I rushed out of my room and practically stepped into the sea. I could see nobody about but I managed to get aboard a raft which floated off the fore end of the Promenade Deck on the Starboard side. One of the stewards managed to reach the same raft and we were both carried under by the suction of the vessel sinking. On reaching the surface four other men swam to the raft where we all hung on until picked up by a Corvette.*

Assistant Steward Harold Hughes found the main staircase had collapsed in a mass of flames after the first torpedo had hit the vessel. He assisted one Wren to a raft on the promenade deck but thereafter lost sight of her. Other survivors testified to the terrifying last moments of the *Aguila*. One nineteen-year-old steward had been blown from his bunk into the companionway by the blast of the first explosion and was saved only because the sudden uprush of water as the vessel was struck by the second torpedo had carried him through a hatchway into the sea. He broke both his legs in the process but he survived. Another man jumped for it as the ship disintegrated beneath him. One man was in a lifeboat which broke up as the ship foundered, flinging him into the water, where he made for a nearby raft. A number remembered nothing from the explosion until they were picked up.

There were only sixteen survivors, including the master, the chief officer John Howel and five other crewmen. Ten of the survivors were clinging to the same raft for an hour-and-a-half until they were picked up by the corvette, HMS *Zinnia*. (It was this corvette upon which Nicholas Monsarrat based HMS *Compass Rose* in his famous novel, *The Cruel Sea*, in which the events of this terrible night are also recognisable.) All the Wrens had lost their lives. The cabins they occupied had been on the port side of the ship and most of them must have been killed instantly when the torpedoes struck the vessel. Sixty other passengers had died including the commodore, three of his staff and the five naval gunners. Sixty-three crewmen had also been killed. These included the chief engineer and the bosun, as well as sixteen-year-old galley boy Gordon Parr, seventeen-year-old steward's boy Fred White and two eighteen-year-olds, a Glaswegian ordinary seaman, Roderick MacRae and an assistant steward John Copley. One hundred and forty-five men and women had lost their lives in the space of two minutes.

It was the loss of the Wrens aboard the *Aguila* which had the greatest emotional impact. Frith, who aged considerably as a result of the sinking of the ship, could never bear to refer to the event afterwards. He always recalled the curious words spoken to him by one young Wren only hours before the ship sank, when she had turned to him to say goodnight, adding "But this is goodbye for me, and I wish you all the luck in the world, but you don't need my good wishes – you'll survive."

The Admiralty finally changed their archaic rule forbidding the carriage of women aboard warships as a result of the loss of the Wrens. The next contingent of Wrens, who were sent out to Gibraltar to replace those lost on the *Aguila,* travelled on board a naval destroyer.

The nightmare that was convoy OG 71 did not stop there. Before the remnants of the convoy reached the safe haven of Gibraltar, six more vessels were sunk, all during the night and early morning of 22 and 23 August, with the loss of almost another 150 lives. The vessels sunk included, most poignantly, the *Empire Oak*. Of the twenty-three who died aboard the *Empire Oak*, six were survivors from the *Aguila*, including Chief Officer Howel. In due course, following the triumphant return of the Nazi U-boat pack to its base at Lorient, on the occupied French west coast, Kapitanleutnant Adalbert Schnee, commander of the U-201 which had torpedoed the *Aguila*, was awarded the Knight's Cross of the Iron Cross, while Oberleutenant Reinhard Suhren of the U-564 which had killed the six survivors of the *Aguila* when torpedoing the *Empire Oak*, was awarded the Oak Leaves to his Knight's Cross. Both survived the war.

Those lucky enough to have been aboard the *Zinnia* were landed at Gibraltar on 28 August 1941. They deserved better treatment than they received after their ordeal. At the shipping office they were kept waiting until eleven in the evening and then they were sent to the Victoria Hotel, "which

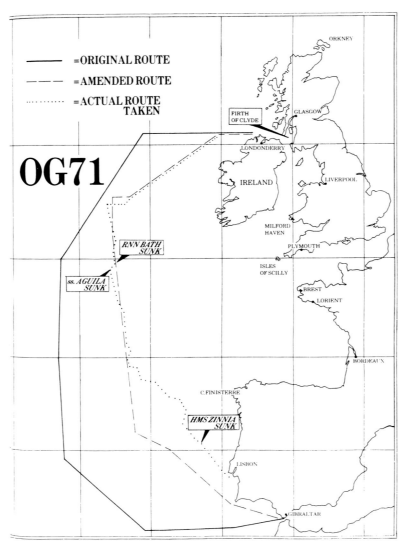

The route of Convoy OG71 – August 1941.

was a filthy place and the food very bad". Arthur Frith reported that they had even had to buy their own soap and carry water into their rooms.

Even now the ordeal of Capt. Frith had not ended. The survivors were sent home on ships of other convoys returning to the United Kingdom from Gibraltar. The convoy upon which Frith was despatched after spending three weeks in Gibraltar was HG 73. He must have had mixed feelings when the ship which he boarded was the *Avoceta*, under the command of Capt. Harold Martin. This too, as the *Aguila* had been, was the commodore ship of the convoy. The *Avoceta* had left Liverpool on 18 August, the day before the *Aguila* was sunk, and had departed from Lisbon for Gibraltar on 13 September. Frith was one of only four passengers the *Avoceta* was able to take on board at Gibraltar since she was already crowded with British and allied refugees she had collected from Lisbon. Carrying seventy crew and eighty-eight passengers, she left Gibraltar in convoy with twenty-four other vessels on 17 September 1941.

Sailing in the convoy HG 73 was as much a nightmare as OG 71 had been. The U-boats hunting in a pack repeated the tactics which had brought such destruction to OG 71. The convoy was shadowed by a German Focke Wulf on 18 to 19 September and by an Italian submarine between 19 and 21 September. On 21 September the naval escort *Vimy* engaged a submarine and the following day the convoy was re-routed further west in an attempt to avoid the U-boats. On 22 to 23 September the Focke Wulf returned and the Admiralty reported that the Italian submarine had again been seen covering the convoy. The Admiralty warned the convoy at 16.47 on 24 September that U-boats were "still in their vicinity". Two hours later, the convoy made a "very drastic jink to the West to attempt to shake off U-boats known to be shadowing".

The carnage began on the early morning of 25 September and only ended three days later. In all, nine merchantmen were sunk, including four which had survived OG 71, as well as HMS *Springbank*, a merchantman converted into a fighter catapult ship. Five of these vessels were lost in a single day, on 25 September 1941, and one of them was the *Avoceta*. She was torpedoed at 3 a.m. and sank with the loss of forty-seven crew and seventy-six passengers. Both Capt. Martin and Capt. Frith were amongst the survivors. Captain Martin lost his second and third officers, his chief engineer, his bosun and two of the youngest members of his crew, eighteen-year-old galley boy Philip Fitzmaurice and sixteen-year-old cadet William Marsden. Second Radio Officer James Stanley, who drowned on board the *Avoceta*, had been serving aboard the *Alfred Jones* when she had been sunk earlier in the year. He was two months short of his eighteenth birthday. The list of passengers lost is heart-rending to read. The loss of the *Avoceta* devastated whole families. The wife and three of the daughters of RAF Sergeant Crutchley were drowned. Only seventeen-year-old Edith Crutchley survived, brought into Liverpool on board the *Starling* with another surviving passenger, Jeannine Nicholson, whose fourteen-month-old daughter, Nelly, had been the *Avoceta*'s youngest casualty. Mrs Ida Barker, from Weymouth, her four daughters aged between fifteen and eight and her three sons aged from seven years to fifteen months, all lost their lives. Seven members of the Newton family were lost, five members each from the Goddard family from Gloucester and from a family of Polish refugees, the Gosiewskas, four from the Cassells family and three from the Dunlop family. These seven families accounted for nearly half the number of passengers lost.

The Mersey-bound part of the surviving convoy reached Liverpool on 1 October 1941. For Arthur Frith, it finally brought to an end a nightmare which had lasted six weeks. For Raymond Yeoward, the loss of these vessels and the loss of so much human life, especially the contingent of twenty-two young Wrens, had a great impact and contributed considerably to his worsening health. Yet throughout such terrible times, he was a tower of

s.s. Avoceta at Coburg Dock, Liverpool c. 1935.

strength and it was typical of him that, without a word to anyone, he should visit the families of the bereaved to express his sympathy. Although he was often misunderstood because of his characteristic quiet reserve, he always had a personal affection for all those he employed.

Captain Arthur Frith.

The only Yeoward vessels now remaining in active service were the *Ardeola* and the *Alca*. The latter was relatively safe in Icelandic waters. The *Ardeola*, on the other hand, remained engaged on convoy duty and the evacuation of refugees. In April 1941, for example, she apparently carried 275 passengers on board from Lisbon to Gibraltar, or nearly two-and-a-half times her peacetime capacity. This run continued until the autumn of 1942 when the *Ardeola* embarked upon her most extraordinary voyage.

On 21 October 1942 the *Ardeola*, unarmed and camouflaged and under the command of Capt. George Affleck, left Liverpool in convoy carrying 2,100 tons of food and general stores and fifty-five crew, including four army gunners, six naval gunners, two signalmen and Lieutenant Hogg of the Royal Naval Reserve. The convoy sailed first for the Clyde and then headed for the Straits of Gibraltar. From Gibraltar, the *Ardeola* and another vessel, the *Tadonna*, were to leave the convoy to undertake special operation "Cropper", running stores to the beleaguered island of Malta, disguised as neutral ships. This was a critical stage in the war and the dangers of sailing across the Mediterranean can be judged from the fact that from June 1940, with the defeat of the French and the entry of the Italians into the war, all British shipping to Egypt, India and the Far East went round the Cape until May 1943. There was another factor which made the *Ardeola*'s task even more difficult. One naval officer serving in the signals division of the Admiralty at the time had heard about the operation and had at once protested to his senior officer "pointing out the distinctive appearance of Yeoward ships which could not possibly be mistaken for anything else". This objection was reported to the Director of Operations (Foreign) but dismissed out of hand.

The two vessels left the convoy on 7 November 1942, thirty miles north of Algiers, but Affleck never saw the *Tadonna* again and the *Ardeola* proceeded by herself. The following day she raised the French flag, gave herself a French name and a French flag was painted on her side. On the evening of the same day she changed to Italian colours, Italian markings were painted on the forecastle and she hoisted the Italian flag. By that time, however, she had already been sighted by a number of enemy aircraft although they had not attacked her. Early on the morning of 9 November, at about 6 a.m. the *Ardeola*, hugging the North African coastline, rounded Cape Blanca from Ras Enghela, inside territorial waters. She was picked up by a searchlight from the shore and received a signal to stop. The *Ardeola* ignored the signal. An hour later, an armed trawler signalled to the steamer to flash her name. The *Ardeola* ignored this request as well. The trawler put a shot across her bows and repeated the signal. George Affleck later reported that "I thought it wise to comply, so pulled the Italian flag down, put up the British ensign and signalled our name".

The trawler signalled to the *Ardeola* to proceed to Bizerta for examination and an armed guard of six Frenchmen was put aboard her. The steamer was now at rest in the Bizerta anchorage. The pleasant French officer in charge of the boarding party enquired about the vessel's cargo and destination and, upon being told, said that permission to proceed was necessary. At 11.30 a.m., however, a naval commander with a much larger armed guard came aboard and took over the vessel, giving the crew half an hour to leave.

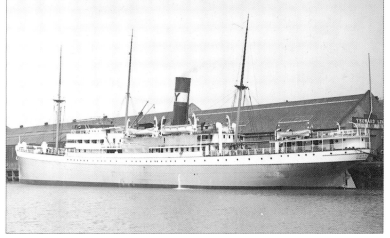

s.s Alca at the Yeoward berth, Coburg Dock, Liverpool c. 1935.

Overnight the *Ardeola*'s crew was housed in the barracks at Bizerta, the officers being taken to one building and the men to another. There they were surprised to be joined at midnight by the crew of the *Tadorna*, which had been captured several hours after the *Ardeola*. On the following afternoon, the two captains were interviewed by the Port Admiral's Chief of Staff whose first words were "I did not feel very well about it when I was taken out of my ship and put in camp at Liverpool". This was not an auspicious start. The officer conveyed clearly to the two men that their every move had been monitored and that their arrival had been expected. He concluded by saying that proceeding to Malta was not possible and, as they were now prisoners of war, they would all be transferred to a camp at Sfax where other British prisoners were held. There they arrived the following morning but only thirteen hours later, at 10 p.m. Capt. Affleck and the captain of the *Empire Defender*, another captured ship, were interviewed by the mayor and the camp governor. They were told that since France was no longer at war with Britain but was now an ally, they would all be set free.

The next morning some 320 British seamen set off in a train composed of iron-ore trucks with a French army lieutenant as their guide to try and reach the British forces in Algeria. This "very long and arduous trip" took twelve days by train and on foot before the men arrived tired and hungry in Algiers at noon on 24 November. They boarded the waiting *Orontes* straight away and had a blessedly uneventful journey to Gourock where the ship arrived on 2 December. Fortunately Capt. McPhee, Yeoward Line's marine superintendent, had gone there to meet them (the only crew who were met or who got ashore that day) and with great persistence in dealing with the Admiralty Berthing Officer, he eventually got on board, collected the crew and persuaded the ABO to take them ashore in his launch. He then had a train held up at Gourock in order to take them to Glasgow, where he arranged accommodation on the night train for Liverpool and they all arrived safely there next morning.

Raymond Yeoward had his own views on the real nature of operation "Cropper". He wrote to his marine insurers requesting a war risks claims form on the day the *Ardeola*'s crew returned to Liverpool, adding:

> *To send a ship alone and unarmed, camouflaged to represent a French ship – the camouflage was laughable – sailing under false colours for scores of miles within sight of the coast and about which the enemy apparently knew all there was to know, appears on the face of it to be such a crazy adventure that one cannot help thinking that she was never expected to reach Malta ... it would seem that the real intention was to send the ship to Tunisia to see what sort of reception she would get. It would not need more than average intelligence to guess what the result would be. The temptation to loot 2,000 tons of foodstuffs would have been irresistible. To the Germans, who are also desperate for food, she must have been a Godsend.*

The *Ardeola* herself was handed over to the Germans by the Vichy French, renamed the *Aderno* and was used as a transport ship in the Mediterranean until the British submarine *Torbay* sank her two miles off Civitavecchia, on the west coast of Italy, on 23 July 1943.

Meanwhile, the sense of comradeship within Yeoward Brothers continued. In all senses, it was and remained a "Family Firm". News still travelled painfully slowly, however. A whole month after the safe arrival of the crew back in Liverpool, a letter to Head Office from Las Palmas branch stated that "the absence of news regarding Capt. Affleck is upsetting", but just another nine days later Clark was able to write from Tenerife on 11 January that he "has heard that Affleck has arrived safe and sound but without luggage".

It was at that same time that an open lifeboat arrived in Puerto de la Cruz carrying nineteen men from a British steamer which had sunk off Madeira. They had been drifting for fourteen days following compass and steering failures and the first thing sighted by one of the survivors warmed his heart – the name "Yeoward" painted in large letters on the side of the packing-house. He was an Irish deckhand, whose home was at the Dingle, Liverpool, and he naturally knew the name well.

Another interesting event which occurred in 1943 was an auction sale in London with the proceeds going to War Charities. One solitary banana brought the incredible price of twenty-eight shillings!

By this time, the loss of life and ships and the strain of running the business almost single-handed, were taking their toll of Raymond Yeoward's health, even though he was ably assisted by George Simpson, his right-hand man since the retirement of Joseph Wardle. Raymond was also concerned about two other issues at this time in the war. The first stemmed from the fact that his mother, Bertha, because of the war and the strict exchange controls imposed by the Spanish government, was unable to derive any income from the Canary properties which his father Richard had retained outside the Partnership and had settled on her for life. A sale of that Canary property would not have prevented a continuation of the business in the Islands, apart from the farming activity which would probably have disappeared, but it would have enabled Bertha Yeoward to enjoy the remainder of her life without financial worries and would also have facilitated the eventual distribution to her family of the proceeds of those assets. Furthermore, it could have relieved the Firm of two liabilities – the maintenance of the farms in the inaccessible Canary Islands and the need for Raymond, its sole proprietor, in his capacity as elder son, to provide for the entire financial needs of his mother. Thus there were many logical reasons to favour the idea of a sale of the assets which did not form part of the Firm. William Clark in fact opened negotiations with one possible purchaser and these lasted many months, during which time correspondence from Raymond highlighted his overriding consideration for all the staff who would lose their employment and "should be generously compensated" (there were no effective social laws in those days!). However, as soon as it was discovered that the purchasing syndicate was "a Spanish concern but with German backing", negotiations were abruptly broken off. The Canary Islands had always been a small community and no secrets remained secret for long – any whisper that "Yeowards are considering selling" was liable to produce a hoard of "bargain hunters", highly detrimental to the business. No further enquiries were therefore entertained.

The second issue which gave Raymond cause for concern came from the fact that the Yeoward Line Ltd. debenture issue had been fully repaid by the first half of 1943. Raymond's brother and sister continued to press for further realisation of their share of the assets of that Company as a result of which, in May of that year, the capital was further reduced by a repayment to shareholders at the rate of £80 per share. This represented yet a further drain upon the liquidity of the business and again took place at a time of great financial uncertainty.

As the war came to an end, the Yeoward business had been run down at home because of state controls. Head Office accommodation was unsatisfactory and the Firm was staffed with ageing employees. Abroad, the fruit business was beginning to recover but the bulk of any profits had to be retained in the Islands. The Ministry of War Transport had employed Yeoward Brothers as shipping managers to manage several vessels (including the Danish fruit carrier, *Slesvig*, which survived to be handed back to her owners after the liberation of Denmark) and on the day following victory in Europe, Capt. Frith was sent to Scotland to take command of one of the German merchant ships surrendering to the Royal Navy. She was renamed the *Empire Lea*, the first of several such "Empire" ships to be commanded by Capt. Frith while being operated by the Yeoward Line on behalf of Sea Transport. But the Yeoward Line itself had lost all but one of its vessels, the *Alca*, and that had been knocked around so much while on duty in Icelandic waters that she would require a complete refit before she could be returned to the Canary route.

chapter five

1945–1959

EVER since the sinking of the *Aguila* in 1941, with the loss of all twenty-two young Wrens on board, it had been the desire and intention of many to commemorate their memory by the provision of a lifeboat for the Royal National Lifeboat Institution (RNLI) but this had not been possible during the war and immediate post-war years. At last, on 28 June 1952, the *Aguila Wren* was launched, and handed over to the RNLI at Aberystwyth at a service attended by the families of the women who had given their lives. Also present at the ceremony were the former Director of the Wrens who had personally selected them for the fateful posting and representatives of Yeoward Brothers including Capt. Frith himself, for whom it was a particularly distressing occasion. During her service with the RNLI the *Aguila Wren* was destined to save a total of thirty-eight lives – a worthy memorial for the twenty-two young ladies who had given their own lives in the service of their country.

The *Aguila*, the *Avoceta* and the *Ardeola* were never replaced by the Yeoward Line. The Government had introduced a scheme for selling government-owned vessels to private owners for fleet replacement. These ships were sold at cost less depreciation with delivery at the end of the war. When a ship was lost, the owner was paid immediately the ship's value, based upon its depreciated historic cost, as at 1939. A second sum, worth about one quarter of the first sum, to cover the increased wartime insurance values of the ships, was credited to the owner but not released until a lost ship was replaced. Any credits remaining seven years after the war had ended would be cancelled. During the war nearly nine million tons of commercially-owned British shipping were lost and more than £268 million was recovered by owners. It can be assumed, therefore, that any sum the Line obtained from the Government could have been sufficient to replace the lost vessels, if the Line's depreciation reserves were adequate.

The main question, however, was whether or not there were sufficient liquid reserves within the Yeoward Line Ltd. to make complete replacement feasible, given that £360,000 had been paid out in cash to shareholders in

1943. Judging from the strength of the Line's liquid assets, it could be suggested that at least partial replacement was possible. Another equally relevant question is whether there was sufficient will to see a full fleet of Yeoward-owned ships sailing to the Canaries again, bearing in mind the complete lack of interest in the Line from any of the major shareholders other than Raymond Yeoward. The deciding factor, however, was probably grave doubts about the future of Canary imports into the United Kingdom in view of the uncertainty that existed at the end of the war. While government controls upon the import of bananas were not lifted until the end of 1945, the market for Canary bananas in Britain must have appeared limited. Nor was it as easy for Yeoward to obtain Canary produce since the system of consignments from individual growers had been superseded by a system of annual contracts for the shipment of bananas under the supervision of the State marketing body, CREP. Far better then for the Yeoward Line to conserve its liquid assets and to supplement the slow and ageing *Alca* with other chartered vessels if necessary.

It is interesting to note that, according to George Simpson, the

Plan of Coronation Naval Review, June 1953, showing s.s. Alca at station at extreme lower left.

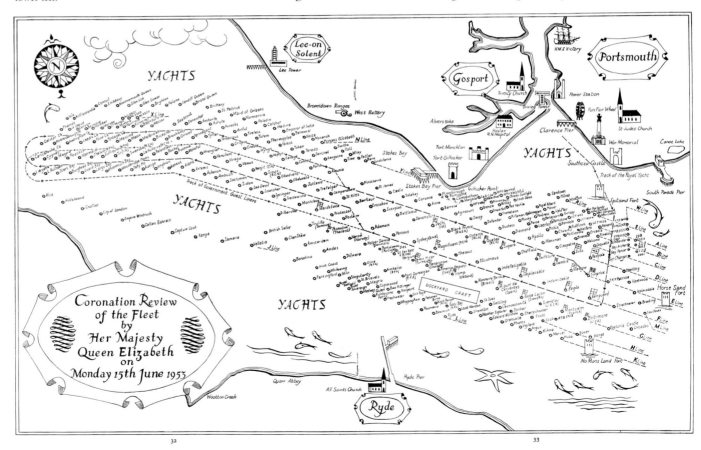

Government had intended to allocate four modern oil-burning German vessels, overhauled and refitted, to the Yeoward Line, which would have enabled a resumption of the pre-war Canary service. Apparently this did not happen because they were handed over to the Russians as part of a reparations agreement.

The *Alca* reappeared in the Mersey on 15 May 1946 in her well-known Yeoward colours, when, with a complement of seventy-eight passengers she embarked upon the first post-war Yeoward cruise to the Canaries. This was the Indian summer of the Yeoward Line. For nearly eight years the *Alca* sailed to and from Liverpool for the Canaries on a monthly voyage lasting nineteen days with five days spent in the ports of call. Fares were now rather higher, ranging from eighty guineas to one hundred guineas per passenger. The *Alca* also had the honour of being one of only twenty-nine merchant vessels in the Coronation Naval Review off Spithead in June 1953. In early 1954 she sailed to the Canaries for the last time. That summer she was chartered to the Danish Government for passenger service between Denmark and Greenland. When that charter ended, she was laid up at Birkenhead before being sent to the ship-breakers at Preston in 1955.

Tony, Raymond's only son, then a schoolboy, sailed on the last of the Yeoward liners twice with his sister and his parents during this period and he kept a diary for both those cruises, the first in April 1947 when he was fourteen years old and the second in April 1950. It was Capt. Frith who had the role of seeing out the last years of the *Alca* as her master. The Mersey was still a river teeming with ships, for Tony recorded, as the *Alca* set sail at

Top: The end of an epoch – s.s. Alca laid up at Preston prior to being broken up – 1955.

Bottom: Passenger photograph of s.s. Alca under Captain Frith in Madeira, April 1947 showing Mr. & Mrs. Raymond Yeoward and their two children.

quarter to ten on 3 April 1947, that she was an hour late "as we were the last in the queue for tugs (there were seven ships sailing that evening)". At Lisbon, the motor cars and vans carried by the vessel as export cargo were unloaded by the ship's crew since the Portuguese dockers were on strike and in the city the sight of shop windows with goods which were actually available for purchase, as opposed to mere dummies, was a sight almost forgotten during long years of war. The *Alca* dropped anchor in Madeira at the same time as the Booth Line *Boniface* homeward-bound for Liverpool. The *Alca* received the same greeting there that had been given to so many Yeoward liners:

> *After dropping anchor we were immediately surrounded by small boats, most of them with samples of native workmanship, mainly wicker-work, to sell and some with small boys waiting to dive for any silver coins. They will not dive for copper coins, so a favourite trick with visitors is to wrap in silver paper a half-penny or penny; one can imagine the boys' faces when they realise that they have been fooled.*

Opposite: Typical voyage chart of s.s. Alca showing the daily distances on which the onboard sweep was based April 1950.

On 16 April the steamer arrived at Santa Cruz where "The very long quay … is usually stacked high with boxes of tomatoes and bunches of bananas, with a congestion of lorries and carts." The ship took on board 300 tons of bananas and 20,000 baskets of tomatoes at Santa Cruz, while at La Palma Tony watched 400 tons of bananas being loaded into the ship. The final port of call before sailing for Liverpool was Las Palmas de Gran Canaria where another 30,000 baskets of tomatoes were loaded.

The cruise taken by the family three years later followed the same route. In Las Palmas one local stallholder refused to take full value for the goods bought by Raymond Yeoward since "he knew to whom he was selling". This time the *Alca* returned to Liverpool without any bananas at all, laden instead with 42,000 baskets of potatoes and 34,000 baskets of tomatoes, "the biggest for some time".

Between ports, life on board followed the same pattern that had been established before the war. On the first day at sea came the election of the sports committee which arranged games like shuffle-board, housey-housey, deck-quoits, whist drives, sweep-stakes and the fancy dress ball which took place on the first night out of Madeira. In the evenings the gong sounded half-an-hour before dinner, which took place at seven. A typical menu was fried fish, turkey and ice-cream. This was followed by an evening sing-song around the piano and the telling of jokes. There was a passengers' concert during which the chairman of the sports committee tried without success "to encourage a rather weak response to the community singing". The cruise taken by the Yeoward family in 1947 coincided both with the birthday of Raymond Yeoward, when the chef baked a special birthday cake, and with

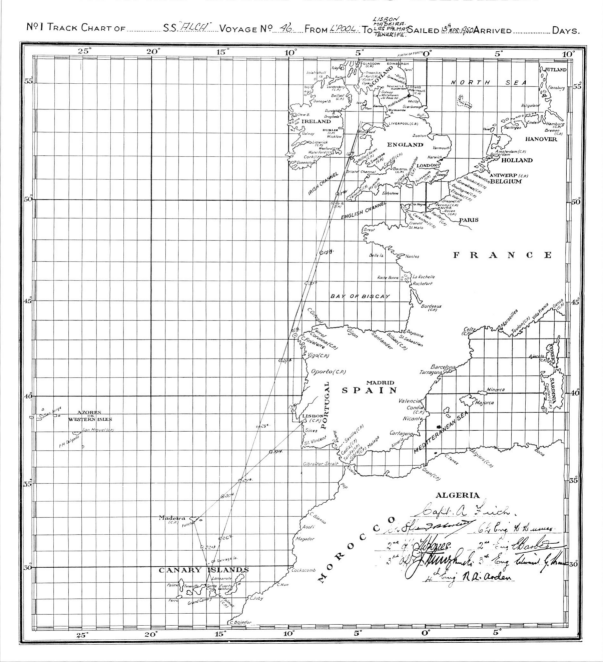

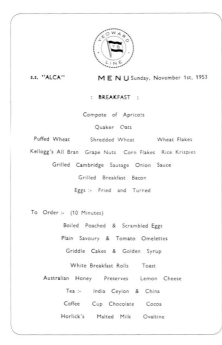
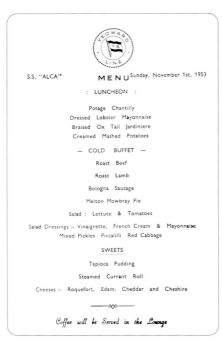

A day's menus from the s.s. Alca, November 1953.

that of Princess Elizabeth, when each passenger toasted the occasion in champagne. On Sundays, a service was held in the dining room.

The weather could, of course, be temperamental. The voyage out to Lisbon in 1947 did not take place in the best of weather for "the rolling of the ship had caused the heavy armchairs and even the sofas to move almost from one side of the room to the other". Never having been abroad nor experienced the open sea, Tony was impressed by his first experience of the Bay of Biscay, not realising that all moveable furniture was secured by chains. The state of health of many passengers was not helped by one elderly man whose jokes were repeated literally *ad nauseam*. In 1950 the rough weather caused a trunk to tip against one cabin wall prompting one elderly man to leap out of bed, thinking that the ship had been hit by a mine.

As Tony's diaries reveal, it was the Canary tomato trade rather than the Canary banana business which was particularly important after the war. But the Canary shippers and growers wanted vessels speedier and better ventilated than the slow old *Alca*. The main reason the *Alca* continued carrying Canary fruit after the war was because there was simply nothing else available in the first instance and the Firm had to protect its Canary berth with whatever was available. For an initial period Raymond Yeoward managed to secure some of the better vessels available on charters of several voyages, before negotiating what was intended to be a longer-term agreement.

When the Yeoward family had sailed to the Canaries in April 1950, they had travelled with a Danish shipowner and his wife, Mr. and Mrs. Christian Clausen. By that time, the Yeoward Line had already entered into an agreement with Clausen whereby his three vessels, the *Dorrit Clausen*, the *Bjorn Clausen* and the *Verna Clausen* (which had limited passenger accommodation) all sailed under the colours of the Yeoward Line carrying fruit cargoes from the Canaries to Liverpool. This agreement operated to the entire satisfaction of all parties, the Canary shippers included, and as a result Christian Clausen was appointed to the Board of the Yeoward Line in 1953. The gap created by the withdrawal of the *Alca* in 1954 was temporarily filled by a chartered Norwegian motorship, the *Prominent*, but the fact that the Yeoward Line no longer possessed any vessels of its own encouraged Clausen to attempt to take over the Canary service on his own. He abandoned the agreement with Yeoward, resigned from the Board of Yeoward Line in December 1955 and persuaded Yeoward Brothers' Liverpool shipping manager, Harry Bradshaw, to desert the Firm which had sustained his employment through many difficult years. But, despite several years' experience, Clausen still failed to wrest the business from the Yeoward Line. This was largely due to the fact that Yeoward Brothers had been established so long in the Islands that they understood utterly the way the islanders operated while Clausen completely failed in this regard.

Clausen's failure was to Yeoward's advantage but it still left Raymond Yeoward without any ships. There was increasing competition on the Canary route from the ships of the Swedish Svea and Express Fruit Lines, the Fred Olsen Line and the Spanish Aznar Line. New arrangements were soon made, however, which again proved entirely beneficial for Yeoward. For three seasons, the Yeoward fruit service was maintained in collaboration with Manchester Liners through the use of the vessels *Manchester Vanguard* and *Manchester Venture*. Neither ship, however, had any passenger accommodation so the cruising business came to an end more than fifty years after it had first begun.

In the Canaries, while more tomatoes were being shipped by Yeoward Brothers to Britain than bananas, it was the latter which were instrumental in returning the Canary business to profit. This was thanks to the constant rise in demand for Canary bananas on the Spanish mainland. In 1946 as many bananas were shipped to Spain as went anywhere else. Ten years later, Spain was taking 53% of all Canary bananas and its share was to rise continuously over the years until Spain and the local market in the Islands accounted for nearly all the bananas produced in the Canaries.

By 1959 Yeoward's banana plantations had been making good profits for several years. Ironically, despite the growing popularity of Canary tomatoes in the United Kingdom, these profits were needed to cover the heavy losses being made by the Firm on its tomato business. Tomato producers insisted upon proceeds in advance which not only tied Yeoward to certain producers but also laid the Firm open to the risk of bad debts as growers either refused to settle any adverse balance or they suffered bad seasons. It is quite probable that Raymond Yeoward sought to avoid these bad debts but several factors would have prevented his success. Yeoward's local management in the Islands was so long-serving and was so used to exercising considerable independence that they had become a law unto themselves. Joseph Wardle's annual visits ended with his retirement in 1939. Thereafter there were no tours of inspection by senior Liverpool management to the Islands during the war and prior to his retirement Raymond Yeoward visited the Canaries only twice after the war, in 1947 and 1950. Without regular inspection it was easy enough for the local managers to persuade Liverpool that they knew best, especially if they did not provide all the information that Head Office requested. During the war, for example, Raymond Yeoward had complained to Clark and Brabyn on numerous occasions that they were not giving him enough information about affairs in the Islands. With part of the banana profits covering tomato losses in the Islands and another part being transferred in the late 1950s to cover losses in the United Kingdom business, the Canary business became heavily overdrawn by 1959.

Mr. & Mrs. Raymond Yeoward in the late 1940s.

In Britain, the revival of the fruit business was not easy. Government control, under the auspices of the Ministry of Food, remained for some time after peace had returned. Although the Ministry began purchasing bananas once again in volume, including Canary bananas, importers of this produce suffered from the poor allocations which were made to them based upon the volumes of the immediate pre-war years. This was because importers were treated on a global basis for allocations, which worked in favour of those importers, like Fyffes, who imported bananas from all over the world and against those, like Yeoward, who had not only been shipping in fruit from a single source but who had also suffered a steep decline in imports from that source by 1939. Yeoward were also disappointed that the Ministry of Food had appointed Elders & Fyffe as the main United Kingdom agent for

1945–1959

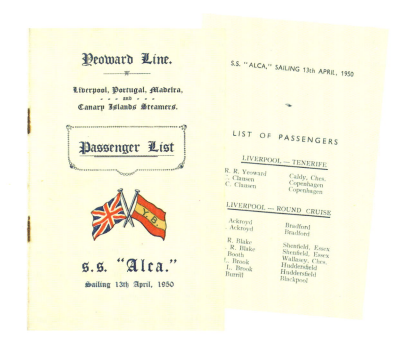

Menu from the Gala Dinner held on board the s.s. Alca at the Coronation Naval Review, Spithead, June 1953.

Passenger list from s.s. Alca April 1950. Passengers included Mr. & Mrs. Raymond Yeoward and their children accompanying Mr. & Mrs. Christian Clausen.

Right: Banana stickers used by Casa Yeoward for promotional purposes in the 1940s.

Below right: Interior patio of the old Puerto office.

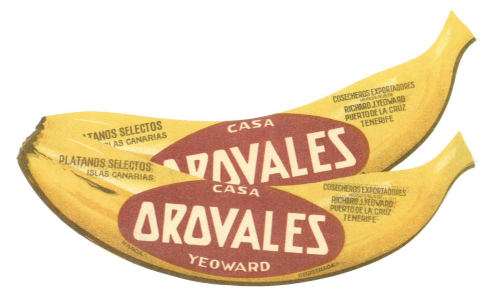

the Canaries and Fyffe's agent in the Canaries as the Ministry's purchasing agent in the Islands. It was also the British Ministry of Food which decided which ships would be utilised for the carriage of bananas and while Yeoward expected that, as a British shipping line, based in Liverpool and using its British registered *Alca*, it might receive preference over foreign lines, this was not the case and in fact preference was instead given to Swedish vessels. It was only after representations had been made to the British Embassy in Madrid that this situation was rectified in favour of the Yeoward vessels. Yeoward was however, appointed by the Ministry of Transport as joint coordinator of shipping bringing bananas into British ports. Yeoward supervised shipping entering Liverpool and other ports on the west coast, while the London agents of Fred Olsen looked after the vessels sailing into London and ports along the east coast.

There was further disappointment in store for Yeoward when State control finally ended. For some strange reason, import licences were to be granted on the basis of the number of hooks traders possessed for hanging bunches of bananas to ripen. George Simpson later wrote: "Never was there such a demand for hooks and surely never can Import Licences have been granted to so many traders who, having received them, had no idea what to do with them. This was something of the *coup de grace* to the legitimate importers of Canary bananas, including Yeoward Brothers."

But the Firm could have no similar complaints over its failure to secure the substantial import licences for apples and pears to which it was entitled on the basis of its considerable pre-war import business, although it had lost most of its records which would have supported this entitlement. When Yeoward's offices had been destroyed during the blitzing of Liverpool in May 1941, so too had most of its records. Whereas other firms in similar situations took the trouble to seek out alternative proof for their claims, the staff at Yeoward Brothers did not, and as a result the Firm was awarded only minimal licences. During many years thereafter, these licences were treated in the trade as saleable commodities and were frequently of very considerable value. This failure cost Yeoward very dearly.

As far as the Liverpool fruit-related business was concerned, bananas made little contribution towards profits generated after the war. These profits came mainly from fees received from the shipping business, under the direct control of George Simpson and from Canary tomato sales controlled by Jim Morley, both of whom spent their entire working life in the service of Yeoward Brothers. During the years 1947 to 1958, annual profits from these activities ranged between £24,000 and £63,000.

The London branch continued to deal in Canary, English and Tasmanian produce. In addition, the branch was involved in produce from

Italy. Particularly important was the beneficial agreement reached with the Dutch wholesale firm of J. Koekoek & Co. under which Koekoek shared Yeoward's under-utilised Covent Garden premises. This lasted until 1966 and the commission and handling charges earned by the branch from business conducted with Koekoek increased branch profits by about one-third on average over this period. The greater part of the remainder of the branch's profits came from the handling of Canary produce, most of which was tomatoes.

The London branch performed consistently well once something like normal trading had been restored after the war. This was in contrast to the other fruit branches at Glasgow, Newcastle and Hull, which all made reasonable profits until the early 1950s, when their performance began to deteriorate to the extent that they were all making large losses by 1959. The good record of the London branch was thanks in particular to the management of Geoff Jones from 1951 onwards. Geoff had joined Yeoward Brothers on 31 December 1948, aged twenty-three, after wartime service in India and an accountancy and business course at the Inland Revenue. He had started at the Firm's branch in Newcastle before moving to London to take over the branch management. Under his management, the branch regularly recorded profits twice the previous post-war average.

He was joined in the London branch on 17 January 1955 by the third generation of the Yeoward family to enter the business. Tony Yeoward had always wanted to enter the Firm and, after he had completed his two years' National Service, it was decided by his father, after consultation with William Clark in the Canaries, that the best thing Tony could do would be to learn Spanish prior to actually joining the Firm's operations. Rather than travelling to the Canaries, where he would probably have spent most of his time speaking English with the managers, Tony went instead to Barcelona and was entrusted to the care of the Firm's long-standing agent there, Antonio Hernandez Cejas. This would also allow him to obtain some experience of how fruit was marketed. What Mr. Clark, based in Tenerife, did not take into account was that in Barcelona, Spanish is a second language, the local population preferring their own Catalan language. The other unforeseen benefit from Tony's stay in Barcelona during 1954 was that he met and fell in love with a young Catalan girl who eventually became his wife two years later.

Once installed in the London branch after his spell in Barcelona, Tony found Geoff Jones an excellent teacher and something of a disciplinarian who would tolerate no nonsense. The young pupil started where training should start – at the bottom. Sticking stamps and making tea soon progressed to the art of filing and to the mystery of accounts; this was interspersed with practical work in the warehouse and with the sales staff. Geoff and Tony were very soon to become close friends, a friendship which would prove as permanent as life would allow. Tony then spent three months at the Newcastle branch under George Fisher, broadening his experience before returning to London. Having completed his National Service relatively recently, when the Suez crisis erupted, it was thought that Tony might be called up for military service again. But to everybody's amazement, it was not him but Geoff Jones – whose service abroad and specialist knowledge of supplies was considered potentially invaluable – who was surprisingly called up at two days' notice. His absence lasted some three months and this proved to be a useful test period for Tony, who was pitched into acting management of the branch without prior notice. Needless to say, he made at least his fair share of mistakes but it was all good experience.

The year 1957 was to witness two further events which could be considered of great significance in Tony's training. The labour force in Covent Garden market, which was highly paid but very unionised, went on strike for almost two full months. For the first few days there was quite a degree of confusion but thereafter the market functioned more smoothly and efficiently than anyone could remember. It was a perfect opportunity for Tony, who still cycled to work every day, to experience at first hand just what was involved on the manual work side (the market was totally old-fashioned with mechanical handling being quite impossible). It proved to be an eye-opener for him, and perhaps for many others, when they realised that the work of almost a week was being completed in a day. The trade unions were never able to maintain the same stranglehold over the market when they eventually returned to work. During this period of training, Tony's first working visit to the Canary branches took place when he travelled to the Islands with his wife. There he was able to meet the Canary management, see the way the branches operated, visit the banana and tomato farms and meet many of the independent growers whose names had become familiar to him during his time at Covent Garden.

The profits made by the Covent Garden branch were particularly welcome to Yeoward Brothers because of the parlous state of the rest of the business by the late 1950s. As well as losses from the other three branches, Cavendish Fruit Stores had been neglected, subjected to poor management and, despite a reduction in the number of shops, had been making losses for a number of years. A further blow came to the Firm from a venture in which it had high hopes. In 1953 it was decided to create another direct source of supply, the same as in the Canary Islands but this time in Italy. The selected area was Cesena, south of Bologna, the centre of an important fruit-growing area specialising mainly in peaches. An Italian subsidiary company, Yeoward

Real Estate S.r.l., was set up and this then acquired a substantial site in Cesena with its own railway siding where a fruit packing-house was built. The idea was sound but its implementation suffered two faults, both relating to personnel. The person put in overall charge was Fred Henson, a trustworthy internal auditor for the UK fruit branches, but whose expertise extended to neither fruit trading nor to international business and much less to the Italian language. In turn, he appointed a Sicilian to be the manager in Cesena. This latter gentleman seemed not to have the slightest intention of using his efforts in the interests of the Firm, being much more active in pursuing his own personal interests and as a result the venture proved to be a trading disaster from the outset. At a time when the rest of the business was in trouble, the losses of £25,000 accumulated by the Italian company up to the end of 1956 could not have occurred at a worse time. It was only thanks to the efforts of Geoff Jones, who was despatched to Italy on a trouble-shooting mission in early 1957, that these losses were stemmed and the business placed on an even keel. The Italian property was leased and eventually sold for a healthy profit in 1965.

The Italian losses came at a time of spiralling financial decline for the British business during the period between 1956 and 1959. In 1956 the Liverpool business made a substantial net loss, the first loss recorded since the war. All the branches except London also made losses as did Cavendish Fruit Stores and the Italian venture. Yeoward Brothers, excluding the Yeoward Line and the Canary business, recorded a net loss of £38,000 in that year. In fact, this pattern was repeated almost exactly over the next two-and-a-half years (the exception being a small profit made by the Hull branch in 1957). The situation was not helped by the need to put aside substantial sums each year to provide for future taxation but it was obvious that the business needed a fundamental reform of the way in which it was being run otherwise the funds being injected into it to keep it solvent would only be wasted. Raymond Yeoward's health had finally been broken by the war and by the unresolved family differences and he recognised that the task of review and reform was too much for him. Instead, in early 1959, he asked his son to undertake this responsibility for in spite of the fact that Tony was only twenty-six years of age at this time, he had already had several years' experience in the business.

chapter six

1959–1979

WHEN Tony Yeoward discovered from his father in February 1959 how critical a state the Yeoward business was in, it was a revelation. He had had no idea at all of the seriousness of the situation. In his own words, it was now "touch and go" as to whether the business could be saved. For a young man only twenty-six years of age, it was a challenging task but he never had any doubts that it should be undertaken.

Tony returned to London for a few days to clarify his thoughts. He took advice from his friend, Geoff Jones, who agreed with Tony that the first step should be to change the status of Yeoward Brothers to a limited company from a sole proprietorship, an outmoded form of operation which had latterly placed too great a burden for its survival on Tony's father.

This step met with the approval of Raymond Yeoward, who agreed to sell the business of Yeoward Brothers to the new company of Yeoward Brothers Ltd. and to become its non-executive Life President. It was decided that the shareholdings in the new company would be distributed between Tony, his wife, his mother and his sister, with a requirement for any directors to take up one of the special class of management shares which had been created. The Board of Directors of Yeoward Brothers Ltd., which began trading on 1 July 1959, would consist of Tony as Chairman, assisted by George Simpson and Geoff Jones as executive

George Simpson, Tony Yeoward and Geoff Jones soon after the formation of Yeoward Brothers Ltd. in 1959.

directors. George Simpson, then aged sixty, had spent all his working life with Yeoward Brothers and had been Raymond Yeoward's trusted right-hand man, especially in more recent years as Raymond's health failed. He brought maturity, experience and an in-depth knowledge of shipping, about which neither Tony nor Geoff had any experience.

The business was sold by Raymond Yeoward for the sum of £76,000. This was essentially the value of the Firm's net assets, but this apparently respectable figure hid a much more serious situation. The Firm had accumulated liabilities of nearly £225,000, of which the overdrawn Canary accounts made up nearly £160,000. While the greater part of the Firm's assets came from funds reserved for taxation which were no longer needed, a significant part of the remainder came from the Yeoward Line Ltd. The decision to wind up Yeoward Line Ltd., as it no longer served any purpose without any ships of its own, had been taken prior to Raymond's invitation to his son to take over the reins of the business.

Raymond Yeoward received the purchase price for the Firm by way of £70,000 shares of £1 in the new Company with the balance remaining as a loan to the Company. Typically, he also insisted that Yeoward Brothers Ltd. should take over a number of outstanding obligations. These included continued superannuation contributions and payment of benefits to retired employees together with the continued employment of a number of staff who might not have been taken on by the new Company on the grounds that they were well over the retirement age or that they would have been considered redundant "on a strictly commercial basis".

This characteristic concern for his employees did have its drawbacks, however. The Board realised that the poor financial situation meant no less than a fight for survival. The shipping was about to disappear completely, the fruit branches were all losing heavily, except Covent Garden, and Head Office had recently won the "Methusela Cup"! This had started as a lighthearted "leg-pull" in the fruit trade in Liverpool, where it was both a matter for admiration and at the same time a standing joke to observe the exceptional loyalty of the Firm's staff. Specifically, at the time of the conversion to Yeoward Brothers Ltd., there were at least six members of staff who had each served the Firm for more than half a century. Most of them had long since passed the normal retirement age of sixty-five and were entitled to their pensions from the Yeoward Superannuation Fund but they neither retired nor were they asked to leave. The new Company adhered to Raymond Yeoward's wishes but persuaded all these elderly retainers to retire during the first two years of the Company's operation, thereby opening up opportunities for younger members of staff.

It was hardly surprising, given the state of the business, that the first fifteen months of the new Company's existence should see a loss recorded of £16,000. It suffered at the time from a lack of sufficient working capital with which to expand the existing business let alone develop new ventures but this did not deter the Board from taking action to tackle problem areas. Tony Yeoward regarded the revival of the business as a long-term project and was determined to place the Company on an even keel within five years. He saw no reason why this should not be accomplished.

There were indeed many problems to be solved in all aspects of the business and the three directors of the new Company worked very closely as a team with complete mutual confidence. It was a hard but a happy time as they struggled to put matters right with George Simpson specialising in shipping, Geoff Jones in fruit and Tony Yeoward having to spend the greater part of his time on Canary Island business, yet at the same time, each covering for the others in all departments.

The London fruit branch, under its new manager John Royle, continued to be profitable, the Newcastle branch maintained a steady business and a new branch was opened in Liverpool. The branch in Glasgow had been a "steady drain" on the business but, rather than close it down, Yeoward reached an agreement in September 1960 with Glass's Fruit Markets Ltd., with branches in Glasgow, Edinburgh and Leith. This was purely a trading agreement whereby Yeoward's Glasgow branch was amalgamated with Glass's and the latter represented Yeoward at its other locations. At Hull, where new management was needed, a similar arrangement was reached during 1962 with R. Wrigglesworth & Son Ltd. Investigations into a similar arrangement in Manchester came to nothing. Nevertheless, certainly within Tony's five-year time-scale, the fruit branches had been turned round, thanks mainly to the efforts of Geoff Jones, and they traded successfully well into the 1970s.

There was, however, little hope for Cavendish Fruit Stores. Unprofitable for years, attempts to revive the business by increasing the number of retail shops failed when the manager appointed to oversee this expansion gave notice after fourteen months and the Yeoward Board decided to cut their losses and sell the business as a going concern. A sale was completed in 1961 which gave Yeoward a capital surplus of £10,000, but not before the manager had absconded with several hundred pounds.

It was also largely thanks to Geoff Jones that the Company weathered the ups and downs of the general fruit trade in the 1960s rather better than some others in the trade. The main areas in which Yeoward traded were Canary bananas and tomatoes, Tasmanian pears and apples, Egyptian oranges, onions and potatoes, as well as fruit from America and Canada, Spain, Italy and the United Kingdom.

Bananas were still coming into the United Kingdom from the Canaries at this time and in 1961 Yeoward joined the newly-formed UK Group of Canary Banana Importers. Yeoward had been initially reluctant to join because of Fyffes' membership but did so at the behest of CREP. By this time, however, the market for Canary bananas in the United Kingdom was quite small and the Group was disbanded two years later. On the other hand Canary tomatoes remained important, contributing some 25% to 30% of the Company's total income in the early 1960s.

As far as the Tasmanian trade was concerned, it was decided that Yeoward should pursue a policy of handling consignments only, thus avoiding the risks involved in merchanting on the Company's own behalf. When Geoff Jones visited Tasmania in early 1962 to develop links with fruit-growers, not only was it the first time that Yeoward Brothers had sent anyone out there, but it was also the first time that the United Kingdom fruit importers had sent anyone to visit the fruit-growers themselves rather than the Australian exporters in their city offices. This made an excellent impression and, with Tony Yeoward making a subsequent visit, the volume of Tasmanian packages handled on consignment rose from 25,000 in 1959–1960 to 100,000 in 1961–1962 and continued to grow in future years.

In England, Yeoward Brothers had dealt individually for many years with a number of fruit growers in Kent. In 1963 this relationship was enhanced when Markads Ltd. was formed. This company, formed under the aegis of and administered by Yeoward Brothers Ltd., brought together these individual growers for the organised marketing of their fruit through Yeoward's sales network. This was the idea of Geoff Jones and it grew steadily until it became independent in the 1980s when Yeoward was on the verge of withdrawing from the fruit trade.

During the 1960s there were a number of occasions when the fruit trade in general suffered terrible losses as a result of disasters occurring at various times and in various sectors of the trade. But Yeoward Brothers Ltd. was able to weather all these crises and usually end up with a profit at the end of the season through its skilful management and through having several different sources for its produce. Indeed, the Company had returned to profit in 1961–1962 and had wiped out the accumulated loss on the profit and loss account by 1965–1966. This was a considerable achievement and the part played by Geoff Jones in this revival was recognised when he was appointed the sole Managing Director in 1966 following the retirement of George Simpson from his executive duties.

Under Yeoward Brothers Ltd., the shipping business had not got off to a good start. While the arrangement between Yeoward Brothers and Manchester Liners had been very remunerative in terms of fee income for Yeoward, it had only yielded losses for Manchester Liners. As it happened, the bid made by the two companies for the Canary Islands–Liverpool shipping service for the 1959–1960 tomato season was unsuccessful. It was won jointly by the Spanish shipping line Naviera Aznar, and by Fred Olsen, both of which had previously competed with each other only on the Canary run to London.

This turn of events left Yeoward bereft of its traditional shipping role. Instead, the Company turned to shipping agency. Aznar's Liverpool agents had been the long-established and well respected firm of Bahr, Behrend & Co. who had acted for Aznar for many years. Nevertheless, Yeoward was able to obtain the Liverpool agency for the Aznar vessel allocated to the Canary–Liverpool service, the ageing *Monte de la Esperanza*, while Bahr, Behrend was left to handle any other Aznar vessels which might come to Liverpool. This was thanks partly to Yeoward's expertise in the Canary tomato trade and partly to the friendly relations which Raymond Yeoward and Don Eduardo Aznar had enjoyed for a number of years.

Yeoward had nothing to lose and everything to gain. No matter how decrepit the vessel, the *Monte de la Esperanza* was a ship, it brought fruit cargoes and it could carry about ten passengers, albeit in "less than luxury". Additionally, its Basque Captain San Salvador, together with his Valencian chief officer Vicente Mirallaves, proved to be the perfect substitute for all the failings of the old ship, at least so far as the passengers were concerned. It was a far cry from the Yeoward Line ships but it was a chance and Yeoward grasped it. Every second Sunday throughout the winter at least one – and if available all three – of the directors of the new Company were on duty on the dockside, supervising the discharge and delivery of the fruit and attending to the requirements of the ship and her master. Thus a close working relationship developed and this was to prove its value over the next two decades.

This hard work bore fruit the following season when Aznar was awarded the entire contract to the exclusion of Fred Olsen, partly thanks to the close personal friendship between Eduardo Aznar and General Franco. The dependence of the service upon this factor always made its future somewhat uncertain, no matter how successful it appeared to be, and increased the element of risk in Yeoward's reliance upon this single line as its sole source of business. Nevertheless, the *Monte de la Esperanza* was joined in service by the fast modern motorship, *Monte Arucas*, which carried thirty-six passengers in comfortable accommodation, and the two ships combined to provide the scheduled weekly service. Yeoward replaced Bahr, Behrend entirely and the new Aznar vessel was consigned specifically to Yeoward Brothers Ltd. Here was another opportunity.

Yeoward was back into the shipping and cruising business and better still, there was consideration of maintaining a year-round service. Naviera Aznar had not previously been involved with carrying southbound cargo from the UK to the Canaries but was persuaded that with Yeoward's established connections in such traffic, an interesting business could be built up provided a regular service was offered throughout the entire year. With a regular weekly service, sailing every Tuesday and arriving back at the modern Kings No. 2 Dock on the Saturday night or Sunday morning tide, the Company could offer return outward cargo to the market and the passenger business, together with cruising holidays, could be revived. The new decade was destined to be a period of rebirth and growth, out of the ashes of what had gone before.

In the 1960–1961 season Yeoward's shipping business returned to profit once more, thanks not to the shipping agency but to the passenger and outward cargo businesses. The Company gave so much energy and enthusiasm to its efforts to increase cargo and passenger bookings that their success persuaded Aznar, at Yeoward's behest, to go one step further. In 1961–1962, the *Monte Anaga*, a vessel of 6,852 tons which had been built in 1959 with accommodation for 100 passengers, was introduced on the service to replace the *Monte de la Esperanza*. This vessel proved so successful with passengers that Aznar again took Yeoward's advice and extended the service from the tomato season in the winter months to cover the summer cruising season. To cope with the flourishing passenger business, Yeoward opened a specialist passenger booking office at Stanley Street in Liverpool under Ralph Salisbury, who had been the Firm's passenger manager during the final years of the *Alca*.

In 1961 the shipping business had appeared to be broadening its horizons when the Company also obtained the Liverpool agency for Bonny & Co., a Spanish shipping firm newly established by Antonio Bonny in the Canaries to carry fruit to the United Kingdom. Tony Yeoward and his wife attended the launching in Holland of the two new vessels, the *Golden Comet* and the *Silver Comet*, which operated the service. Unfortunately it was unsuccessful and the service lasted only two seasons.

On 27 October 1965 Raymond Yeoward's health finally gave up. The family business to which he had dedicated his life had been restored to a position of growing strength by the time of his death at the age of sixty-nine.

Three months later, on reaching his sixty-seventh birthday, George Simpson retired after more than half a century of active service, having placed the shipping fortunes of the Company onto a firm foundation. He agreed, however, to continue as a non-executive director for another three years – and indeed, he retained his close personal interest in the fortunes of the business until the end of his life.

Following his retirement, the Board was strengthened by the appointment of John Royle as a director on 1 January 1969. John was the manager of the London branch and his appointment coincided with the seventy-fifth anniversary of the founding of the business.

By the late 1960s, through their established relationship with Aznar, Yeoward could again offer passengers cruise holidays under the slogan "Sunward by Yeoward". In 1967 passengers had the choice between a holiday of eighteen days (including eight nights in a Las Palmas hotel) from £85 to £105 per person or a holiday of twenty-five days (including fifteen nights in a hotel) from £95 to £130 per person. These holidays were so popular that, by the 1968 season, passenger demand had outgrown the capacity of the *Arucas* and she was replaced by the *Monte Umbe*, a vessel of the same age but, at nearly 10,000 tons, with accommodation for 360 passengers. She had previously been intended for the Aznar service between Spain and South America. At the same time Yeoward had not forgotten the fruit cargoes involved on the route and in the same season completely palletised inward and outward cargo services were introduced between Liverpool and the Canary Islands. This was handled at a new Liverpool berth, North 2 Kings.

Monte Umbe c.1968.

Naviera Aznar had its own offices in the Canary Islands and therefore the relationship, which had been established so satisfactorily in Liverpool, was not extended to cover the Islands. This, of course, meant that Yeoward no longer needed to employ as many staff in its own offices in Las Palmas and Santa Cruz and these were substantially reduced. This was just one of the many changes that Tony Yeoward was having to make to the operation of the Yeoward interests in the Islands. In fact, he had to make so many visits to the Canaries that in 1964 he decided that a firm grip on the Canary business could only be taken if he and his family went to live there.

There were a number of other reasons why a Yeoward came to reside in the Canary Islands for the first time and it was much to the consternation of the local managers. Over the years, there had been little direct control from Liverpool over Yeoward's management in the Islands, with most of the managers being given authority to manage the business locally as they saw fit. This had created a feeling of total independence not only from Head Office but also between the individual branches and had led to a sense of drift, a breakdown in collaboration and an uncoordinated approach. The arrival in their midst of a member of the family to take up an executive role alarmed managers not only because they would have to defer to his wishes but also because they had tended to become like viceroys – the visible heads of a long-established and highly respected business house, the "Casa Yeoward". This was especially noticeable in the case of the banana-growing branch in Puerto de la Cruz, which itself still remained a small village where everyone knew everyone else and where the manager himself had lived for half a century, most of it as the top man.

As well as trying to impose greater discipline upon the Islands' management, Tony also wanted to settle in the Canaries to take charge of the changed family situation there. Because of the problems created by the civil war, followed by the world war, compounded by the imposition of exchange controls and finally by the demands of the United Kingdom fiscal regulations, the life interest in the Canary properties left by his grandfather Richard to his widow had become a total liability for her. Having for all her life been accustomed to a very comfortable standard of living and in her bereavement and widowhood having been generously and adequately provided for, suddenly within some three years, through no fault of her own, she was being pursued by tax demands for what she "might have had" – but could no longer receive. Naturally this was a combination of circumstances which her family could not allow to continue and so, after taking advice, she renounced her inheritance with the result that her three children became the legal joint owners of the Canary properties as her husband had intended should be the case, but only upon her death. Despite this, it was upon Raymond Yeoward alone that the responsibility had fallen for the care of his mother in her latter years. Moreover, he alone had endured the burden of directing the business during the Second World War and with it the well-being of the staff and their families and it was only when better times returned that his brother and sister had once more become interested in their inheritance. They had clashed continually over the way the Canary properties should be managed and the stress of this had contributed directly to Raymond's failing health and had created a management impasse which left affairs in the Canaries even more in the hands of the local managers than before.

Tony Yeoward only became aware of this family conflict shortly before his father asked him to take over the reins of the business. He realised that a resolution of this difficulty was essential if there was to be a future for Yeoward's interests in the Canaries. By this time, Raymond Yeoward, his brother Bernard and his sister Evaline were so weary of the whole thing that they had decided that the only course of action lay in the disposal of the whole of their interests. They had an ally in this cause in the person of W. A. Clark, the local senior manager. It was through Mr. Clark that negotiations for the sale of the Canary Island properties were conducted. Inevitably, no matter how discreetly he set about trying to achieve this objective, the mere fact of trying to open possible negotiations meant that outsiders would become involved. Therefore it was impossible to avoid staff learning, at least in general terms, what was happening and understandably this undermined their confidence in the future. The decline had set in and was gathering momentum. Well into his seventies, Clark was on the verge of retirement and felt that the end of "Casa Yeoward" would be a simultaneous confirmation of his achievements which would stand for all time, unable to be challenged by any successor.

By 1961 negotiations had reached an advanced stage for a sale to a German who was no fool and could see the opportunity to acquire the whole of "Casa Yeoward" for perhaps less than half a million pounds sterling. Obviously the final details of the proposed agreement would have to be negotiated directly with the family but he had done his homework and knew that this should pose no great problem – the head of the family was a very sick man, none of them had much personal knowledge of the properties or of the day-to-day business as run locally and in fact the only one who knew anything at all about it, or who could speak any Spanish, was Raymond's son Tony – the representative of the incoming new generation. As he was a mere youngster, however, and still lacked experience in business, this should be no obstacle. So the purchaser sent his representative to Liverpool with instructions and authority to negotiate the final price as low as possible. Little did he expect the polite, but total, refusal even to consider any negotiations whatsoever, let alone get down to discussing a possible price. The message from Tony Yeoward was unequivocal – "Casa Yeoward" was NOT for sale.

This announcement also represented a very major reversal of policy within the family and within the Firm. In one deed it broke the local management plan to negotiate a sale and close-down and it cut from under their feet the ideas of the family members to sell at any price. At the same time it created a tremendous moral responsibility for the young Tony Yeoward to resolve the differences which had created the family's wish to get out – a task which at that moment of time seemed a virtual impossibility, Tony himself having already dedicated two fruitless years to it without any noticeable sign of progress.

More than two years then passed during which time Raymond Yeoward, as he had with the British business, made over to his son his business interests in the Islands on 1 July 1962 and their trading name was then changed from "Raymond R. Yeoward" to "Anthony R. Yeoward". There had, however, been no further progress in resolving the difficult family situation although, with two out of the three parties still keen to sell, another offer had been made, investigated and come to nothing. In April 1964 Tony was in Tenerife at the same time as his aunt Evaline and had further discussions with her about the situation. On the day of her departure, she finally agreed to sell her share in the properties provided that two of these were conveyed to her outright.

There are times when decisions have to be taken, sometimes even disregarding the reality of whether one has the legal right to make such decisions. These properties were one-third owned by his uncle Bernard but communications at that time were such that it was impossible for him to be contacted urgently and Evaline was departing early that same afternoon. Tony accepted the offer, not knowing even whether he would have the support or participation of Bernard – in other words, whether he was taking on a commitment to purchase and finance the whole of her interests, or only half, or any other proportion as might subsequently be agreed between Bernard and himself.

Agreeing to meet her an hour later at the airport, Tony went to the office, collected a typewriter and some paper, and told the office driver to take him to the airport. In the car he typed out a form of agreement, setting out the conditions she had determined and which had been agreed verbally. By the time he arrived at the airport, his aunt already had her boarding card in her possession to fly back to England. They both signed the agreement and minutes later her flight was called for boarding.

In those days it was becoming possible to establish international telephone contact but only with very considerable patience. After spending several hours trying to get a telephone call through to England to inform his uncle of the position and to arrange a meeting, when eventually the line was established he was exasperated by the reply: "We are much too busy with the local Pony Club this month; I cannot see you until three or four weeks hence." When he was finally able to visit Bernard the following month, an agreement was reached whereby both would participate in equal half shares of the purchase. At the same time, all the properties now owned jointly by the two men were divided between them at Tony's request so that either one could dispose of his own interests without any of the difficulties seen in the past. Tony drew up a list of properties for this purpose and Bernard decided which he would retain and which would pass to his nephew. In this way, the division was achieved swiftly and without rancour. While the ownership of the properties was divided, however, the control and administration of the business would remain as one, albeit with separate accounts for the two different owners. In fact, this method worked entirely satisfactorily for the next seventeen years.

Since the family dispute had been resolved, Tony decided that the time had come for him and his family to settle in the Islands in order to supervise the changes which would now take place. He subsequently took up residence in Puerto de la Cruz and has continued to live there to the present day although he has always retained the post of non-resident Chairman.

1959–1979

The new Hotel Botanico with the offices of Casa Yeoward in the foreground and Mt. Teide in the background c.1974.

The new hotel in the Botanico estate with banana plants in the foreground c.1974.

The offices of Casa Yeoward situated at the entrance to El Botanico.

The first thing Tony turned his attention to upon settling in the Islands was the loss-making tomato farm in Sardina which continued in business only thanks to an ever-increasing bank overdraft. Two steps were taken to stop these losses. Firstly, Tony realised that land in the Islands now had as much value for property development as for cultivation. He therefore obtained planning permission on a small part of the Sardina farm and sold off the small plots to local people at affordable prices and in easy instalments. This created a positive cash-flow. Secondly, a search began for a tenant for the rest of the farm. In July 1965 a five-year lease was signed with Exportadores de Tomates de Alicante SA, at a good rental, and later that year the proceeds from the sale of the Calderina farm brought a further reduction in the size of the bank overdraft.

The entrance to the La Paz banana plantation showing the farm foreman, as it was when it was opened up for development of the El Botanico estate – 1966.

Tony was also quick to grasp that the Islands' economy was changing. Since the late 1950s, the importance of tourism had been increasing steadily. Growing numbers of visitors were coming to the Islands as the post-war rise in the standard of living in western Europe made foreign holidays in the sun available to more and more people. This was already altering the pattern of employment and making it steadily more expensive to employ labour on the banana farms. Furthermore, the rise in tourism confirmed the trend for the value of land to lie more in its development potential than in its agricultural use. So bananas would become more and more expensive to produce while the land itself could be put to more profitable use.

The outcome of this line of thought was Intercon SA, a Spanish company which Tony established with his brother-in-law, Enrique Morell, in October 1965, with the intention of developing the farm at Llanos de Mendez, although this idea was eventually rejected as being too costly because of the remoteness of the farm. Instead, it was decided to develop the farm at La Paz where the El Botanico estate was to take shape over the next few years, albeit that in order to get free possession of a small cottage in the farm, which had been rented for 37 pesetas per month since decades earlier, Intercon had to build a new house and give the freehold to the tenant – a speedier and cheaper procedure than eviction! The development plans were not entirely well-received by staff who had been brought up to believe that there was nothing more valuable than the banana plant. The foreman at La Paz, who was then approaching seventy years of age and had spent his working life there, wept openly on the morning that the bulldozers began to uproot the plants.

Already by 1966 the bank overdraft had been repaid in full and the account at the bank had been closed following the sale for redevelopment of the Yeoward offices in Puerto de la Cruz. Indeed, the change in attitude on the part of the regional manager of the bank was rather remarkable. For a prolonged period, he had been demanding the clearance of the account, including an ultimatum on the very evening when Tony was on the way to the airport to try to see his father before he died. Now, suddenly, the sun shone brightly once more and "Casa Yeoward" was a "most wanted client" again. Tony closed the account at the earliest opportunity and although the bank had asked the Firm to reopen the account on many occasions since that time, the family have never forgotten their treatment in those difficult times.

The Yeoward packing and transport business operated from the Santo Domingo packing-house in the centre of town and it was becoming ever more inconvenient due to the steady increase in traffic congestion. Once the office had been moved out to the La Paz farm/El Botanico estate, the disadvantages became even more apparent. The then-existing Town Hall of Puerto de la Cruz was situated in an old and dilapidated house in a back street of the town. So the Santo Domingo packing-house property was presented to the Town Council, on condition that the site be used to build a new Town Hall appropriate to the growing importance of the town.

The packing and transport operations were moved to the other warehouse owned by the Firm, conveniently situated on the main road in the centre of the valley. However, with rising costs and reducing volume, the operation was no longer commercially viable and soon afterwards "Casa Yeoward" joined a local cooperative, doubling the latter's output at a stroke.

The profitable policy of redevelopment was also pursued with the site of the Firm's Las Palmas office and warehouses, on which a development of shops, offices and 130 apartments known as Edificio Yeoward was built, the last apartments being sold in 1983.

In the meantime there had also been significant staff changes in the Islands. W. A. Clark had retired in 1961 after his negotiations for the sale of the Canary business had come to nothing. William Shipley took over as general manager for Tenerife. Always in his element when his work involved him directly in the Firm's agricultural activities, it was at this time that Shipley began to experiment with a revolutionary method for the cultivation of tomatoes. This was the "ring culture" system in which the tomato plant was forced to develop two distinct root systems. The system took its name from the bottomless pot, or "ring", of compost which encased the upper part of the root. Controlled doses of fertiliser were applied to this "ring" while the lower part of the root was kept in continuously irrigated volcanic ash. Shipley persuaded Yeowards to purchase land at Candelaria where a commercial "ring culture" venture was set up. The results were astonishing, each plant producing up to forty pounds of top grade fruit as opposed to under two pounds of fruit using traditional methods. The first fruits of this experiment reached Liverpool in 1961 but the experiment was short-lived. Candelaria turned out to be too windy and the plants suffered badly from wind damage over the five or six seasons of the experiment. With funds in short supply and being used for more important matters (the purchase of Evaline Yeoward's share of the Canary properties and the development of El Botanico), the Firm was unable to invest the sums needed to make the experiment a commercial success. At the same time, Shipley was taken seriously ill and returned to England where he died in hospital in 1969.

Jack Hennessey's retirement (April 1976).
From left to right: Geoff Jones, Jack Hennessey, Tony Yeoward, Rex Owens.

In Puerto de la Cruz, Harold Mason and Manuel Abreu had been appointed joint local managers for the Orotava Valley. Mason was a young man who spoke excellent Spanish and was eventually transferred to Las Palmas in 1964 where it was intended that he succeed Victor Allen upon the latter's retirement in 1965. Manuel Abreu was only the second Spaniard to be appointed to the post of manager by the Firm, the first having been Juan Perdomo Aguilar in the 1930s. Rex Owens left Las Palmas for Liverpool in 1962 where he became a valued member of staff as head of the shipping department. He was appointed the Honorary Consul for Spain in Liverpool in 1970 and was decorated for his services in October 1975, when Spain opened a Consulate General in the port. This situation was to be repeated many years later when in 1990 David Bishop was similarly appointed Honorary Consul for Spain in Liverpool.

Tony Yeoward had learned from his father that the business was as much, if not more, about people as it was about profits. The Superannuation Fund his grandfather had begun was modernised in the early 1960s, when a death-in-service benefit and a widow's pension were introduced following the actuary's report of a healthy surplus. Possibly this was the first major change

sunward by yeoward

Left to right: Rex Owens, Cyril Bennett, George Simpson, George Fisher, Tony Yeoward, Ralph Salisbury, John Royle, Jim Morley, Geoff Jones, Jack Hennessey on the occasion of the 75th Anniversary Dinner in 1969.

since its creation in 1916, as another modification was to remove the upper limit on salary levels on which both contributions and pensions would be calculated. This had remained unaltered at £500 p.a. since 1916.

In January 1969, when the Firm celebrated its seventy-fifth anniversary with a dinner at the Blundellsands Hotel in Crosby, Tony Yeoward said:

We are celebrating now our third quarter centenary. But it is the first one which we have been able to celebrate. The first came just after the younger of the two brothers had died, in his forties, and at a time when many of the staff were still away serving King and Country, although the War itself was over. Some would never come back, such as those who went down in no less than five of the Firm's ships lost during the first War.

It was at that time that the Superannuation Fund was founded – at the time a benefit enjoyed only by the staff of a few of the largest public companies.

1959–1979

The second quarter centenary certainly began on a much brighter note than the first had finished on and in no time the colours were flying high again. But history was to repeat itself and the half centenary could not be celebrated. Once again most of the staff were away, fighting for the survival of their country. Once again the losses of the Firm were considerable, the Head Office had been bombed, all but one of the ships had been destroyed and more tragically, many of those gallant people who served the Firm devotedly would never return. By then Mr. Raymond was the sole proprietor, as his father had been 25 years before, and as such he carried a heavy responsibility. I can remember the day when he received the news of the sinking of one of the ships; I don't know which one – I suppose I was about 8 and 9 years old at the time – but the thing which I do remember vividly about that occasion was the effect on him of the loss of the personnel. This is a family Firm and such losses are personal losses.

At such times the family motto has been most appropriate. Literally translated, it means "persevere through difficulties". There have been difficulties, and we have persevered.

So, in a vastly changing world, Yeoward Brothers now celebrates its 75th birthday. As in the past, so in the future, difficulties will arise but we must continue to persevere. Opportunities great and small will present themselves; let us seize them for the benefit of all. Let us now go forward together, as a family, as a team, towards our centenary and beyond.

Perhaps some of you may remember the notice in Mr. Richard's private office which said: "Work 8 hours a day and don't worry; someday you may be the boss, work 12 hours a day, and have all the worry."

Ever since the Firm was founded it has been a Family Firm in which the emphasis has been on loyalty and teamwork. It is thanks to this close collaboration between all members that we have been successful.

YEOWARD BROTHERS LTD.

Dinner Dance

to celebrate the

75th ANNIVERSARY

of the founding of the firm of

YEOWARD BROTHERS

on the

1st JANUARY, 1894

FRIDAY, 3RD JANUARY, 1969
BLUNDELLSANDS HOTEL
LIVERPOOL, 23

Yeoward Brothers Ltd. Dinner Dance Programme for the 75th Anniversary at Blundellsands Hotel, Liverpool, in 1969.

We have decided to introduce a Profit Sharing Scheme, so that henceforth each and every member, no matter how old nor how young, no matter how senior nor how junior, will share directly in the fortunes of the Company, proportionately to their position. For this purpose, a dividend equal to the dividends paid to the shareholders of the parent Company will be paid for the direct benefit of the staff.

This Profit Sharing Scheme had been under consideration for some time and Tony had written to his fellow directors only recently that he hoped such a scheme would encourage both staff and shareholders to focus beyond the short-term, to the Company's medium-term prospects. For the United Kingdom fruit business the 1970s started with the acquisition by Yeoward of a 50% stake in the long-established Liverpool fruit wholesalers, Mark Revill (Liverpool) Ltd., a move which Geoff Jones intended should strengthen the Company's fruit trading operations. In fact this partnership was not an easy one and the Revill stake was sold back to the founding family in 1979. The Company's progress elsewhere was also a matter of swings and roundabouts. The Newcastle branch incurred huge losses in the early 1970s largely due to unauthorised trading and the branch was sold in 1974. The Hull branch was closed when the association with Wrigglesworth ended with the latter's death in 1976. Covent Garden's move to Nine Elms in 1975 boosted Yeoward's London trade but led to the disposal of the Long Acre property after a presence in Covent Garden which had lasted eighty years.

Left to right: Jim Morley, Vic Parry, Jack Hennessey, Geoff Jones (1976).

The shipping business saw the 1970s begin with a dock strike in Liverpool. Without tugmen, the *Monte Umbe* had to be berthed without tugs and worked from the landing stage by Yeoward's own staff, who did an excellent job. The *Monte Umbe*, however, was withdrawn by Aznar from the winter service after the 1969–1970 season because of too little outward freight and limited refrigerated space, together with the fact that there had been too few passengers through the winter. She was replaced in the following winter season by the *Monte Urquiola* but the excellent summer

1959–1979

Monte Urquiola c.1970.

cruise figures allowed Yeoward to persuade Aznar to retain the *Monte Umbe* during the summer and increase the number of cruises from five to eight.

When Liverpool's southern docks system was closed in 1972 and Yeoward moved berths to NE3 Alexandra Dock, they set up a subsidiary company, Port of Liverpool Fruit Terminal Co. Ltd., which negotiated the licensed berth Agreement with the Port of Liverpool Authority. Perhaps the most significant outcome of the new agreement was the construction of a new passenger terminal – an indication of the success of the Yeoward cruises. Indeed, the passenger booking office had now become Hunter Travel Services Ltd. and, under the name of Griffin Travel, a travel agency began operating in Victoria Street in 1973. This was the same year in which the new Alexandra Passenger Terminal was opened and the ceremony on 21 June was attended by Liverpool's Lord Mayor.

The revenue from cruise passengers and cargo freight continued to increase. The cruises remained particularly successful, although Geoff Jones noted in 1972–1973 that there had been a "Bank Holiday panic when the *Monte Urquiola* was one day late from her Scandinavian cruise". During the 1974–1975 season the *Monte Umbe* and the *Monte Ulia*, the replacement for the *Monte Anaga*, had enjoyed continued success but at the end of that season the *Monte Umbe* was sold. This was the first sign that the Aznar Line was beginning to suffer from financial problems. Aznar had been investing heavily, in supertankers and roll-on roll-off ferries, the former to capitalise upon the forecast prosperity of the oil business, the latter to earn a quick profit through resale before they had been completed or paid for. This considerable investment had come at the very moment when the oil crisis of 1972 to 1974

Monte Granada c.1975.

Cruising information issued by Yeowards as agents for the Aznar Line – 1978/9.

occurred, precipitating a world-wide recession as oil prices soared. With no oil for its tankers and no buyers for its ferries, Aznar needed cash and the profitable *Monte Umbe* was the most attractive vessel for prospective purchasers.

This, of course, halved Yeoward's cruising programme at a stroke, although matters improved during the winter of 1975–1976 when Aznar introduced the *Monte Granada* to the service. This modern and luxurious vessel was one of two ordered by Aznar specifically for the UK-Canary Islands routes. Until the *Monte Granada*'s sister ship, the *Monte Toledo*, entered service, however, chartered Russian vessels had to partner the *Monte Granada* and they proved to be less than satisfactory, not only for passengers but also for cargo, in terms of speed and size. It was only in 1976–1977 that the *Monte Toledo* began operating and brought immediate increases in passenger and freight revenue but this improved service did not even last a season. In January 1977 the *Monte Granada* was withdrawn from the service which was then reduced to fortnightly sailings during the summer using the *Monte Toledo* only. Then, at the end of that season, came the news that both vessels had been sold by Aznar to the Libyan Government.

The service stumbled on for another two years, steadily deteriorating. First, Aznar used the unsuitable roll-on roll-off vessels for the service and this attracted considerable criticism. This was compounded by the dock strike at Liverpool at the end of 1977, which prevented the discharge or despatch of the Canary vessel and led the

Canary exporters to suspend shipments to Liverpool. The suspension was lifted a month later only after concerted efforts by Yeoward's staff. The following season, indecision and delays prevented the introduction of chartered vessels until December 1978. All Aznar's subsequent attempts to improve the situation came to nothing as the Aznar Line itself plunged deeper and deeper into financial difficulties. Aznar then failed to regain the fruit service contract for 1979–1980 and, in the late summer of 1979, finally suspended payments. Without the support of Franco, who had died in 1975, there was no hope that Aznar could survive. Their collapse left Yeoward Brothers Ltd., who had prospered from the association for nearly twenty years, once again without a shipping service.

Perhaps the greatest activity within Yeoward during the 1970s came in the Canary Islands. The economy of the Islands was changing, with the emphasis moving away from traditional agriculture towards the development of tourism. Two consequences of this change were the absorption of the cooperative banana packing-house, in which Yeoward was a participant, by Tenerife's largest cooperative packing-house, FAST, in a satisfactory deal, and the collapse into bankruptcy of ETASA, who were tenants of the Sardina tomato farm. The tomato farm found another tenant, Marcelo Baez, a grower and exporter from Las Palmas, who took a lease which lasted for ten years before increasing financial difficulties obliged him to withdraw and the farm was successfully sold.

Tomatoes being unloaded at Liverpool from an Aznar Line vessel, showing baskets and cartons – mid 1970s.

Meanwhile, the development of El Botanico, a high-quality residential estate, had proved itself a total contrast to the low-cost development in the tomato farm in Sardina, Gran Canaria. In view of the financial situation in which the "Casa Yeoward" had found itself when this project was commenced, taking on a new ten million peseta infrastructure-development contract had been a major responsibility and it had meant much hard work. By the turn of the decade, however, it had become universally accepted as the best development in the island – and probably anywhere throughout the Canary Islands.

Following the construction of roads and several groups of bungalows, the first building of residential apartments in the estate was commenced. The opportunity was taken to adopt a policy of recalling the names of the Firm's ships which had been so well known in the Canary Islands in earlier years and, accordingly, the first two groups of apartments were named *Alca* and *Alondra*.

All the streets in the Botanico estate had been given names of trees in order to establish its character with the principal street being *Avenida de las Palmeras*. The Town Council of Puerto de la Cruz, without prior warning of their intention, in a plenary session in 1970, renamed that principal street *Calle de Richard J. Yeoward* in honour of the memory of the founder of the Firm and in recognition of all the benefits which he had brought to the area – a gesture which was much appreciated by the Yeoward family even if it did spoil the botanical intentions!

Meanwhile, Tony had already seized another opportunity which was presented to "Casa Yeoward" as a result of the growing importance of tourism to the Islands, coupled with land that the Firm owned. This was the opportunity to benefit from providing the Islands with their first luxury hotel. In May 1970, Tony, his wife and his brother-in-law met with their advisers and their architect and decided to put in hand the development of the Hotel Botanico. With the participation, as shareholders in the venture, of Naviera Aznar, Juan Gaspart (then Barcelona's leading hotelier) and Catalan businessman Felix Gallardo, a new company, Atlantico Canaria SA, was formed in May 1971 to undertake the project. A further ten months elapsed before plans were approved and construction work was able to begin in March 1972. The next two years was a hectic period, with frequent board meetings (usually in Barcelona for the ease of most of the shareholders), site visits and negotiations to secure the future management of the hotel. This was eventually entrusted to a leading firm of Canary hoteliers, Horesa. The first manager appointed was Adolfo Mathias Gil and he accompanied Tony Yeoward to Britain to order as much equipment as possible for the hotel. Obtaining the goods turned out to be rather harder than ordering them. A typical example related to the silver cutlery for the hotel. In view of the shipping operations run by Aznar and Yeoward, this aspect should have posed no problem as all that was required of the chosen supplier was to deliver the order to Liverpool docks five months later. In the event, the cutlery was four months late and arrived two months after the hotel's opening. These two months included the Christmas season when the hotel was fully booked and in the circumstances cutlery had to be begged or borrowed from wherever it could be found.

The original instructions to the architect had been "to create beautiful gardens – and by the way, include a quality hotel in them!" When it was completed, the hotel's floor area covered seven acres while its gardens covered five and the gardening contractor was the only contractor who fulfilled his contractual obligations to perfection. Not a single one of the many mature trees brought over from the mainland was lost, including varieties of palms and olives, and the completed gardens became one of the hotel's main attractions, gaining widespread plaudits as well as "Protected Area" status when they reached maturity several years later.

Despite the fact that the effects of the world oil crisis of 1973 - 1974 took its toll of the tourism market and soaring inflation added more than half a million pounds to the development costs, the Hotel Botanico actually opened early. It had been intended to open at the end of November 1974 but it was agreed to open at the beginning of the month to accommodate the clients of a particular travel agent. The Belgian couple who were the hotel's sole guests on 9 November 1974 had the attention of the entire staff of more than three hundred employees. The official opening of the hotel took place a month later, over the weekend of 6 to 8 December, when nearly 130 guests from the travel industry stayed at the hotel. At the celebratory dinner, Tony Yeoward again emphasised the human side of the hotel's success, speaking of "the closest collaboration between a few people, Spanish and British, working in complete harmony ... a small united team, a perfect example of Anglo-Spanish collaboration, each applying the age-old formula which carried both our nations to the heights of world supremacy in earlier times: initiative, integrity, hard work and perseverance".

The opening of the Hotel Botanico encouraged Tony to seek the further development of Yeoward's own small interest in the travel business. Yeoward Brothers acquired a majority interest in the London-based Travellers Consultant Services Ltd. and its operating subsidiary, R. M. Brooker Ltd. The discovery of losses during the first year after this occurred led to a renegotiation of the acquisition, as a result of which Yeoward Brothers Ltd. obtained 100% of both companies. Brooker then became the United Kingdom agent for the Hotel Botanico.

A further development came with the introduction on the Canary route of the *Monte Granada* in 1975 and then the *Monte Toledo* in 1976. As the Yeoward Line had pioneered so many years before, so now Yeoward reintroduced the "Sail-and-Stay" holiday, using the two modern Aznar vessels and the Hotel Botanico. Because of Aznar's own troubles, however, this was only short-lived. By then, despite some early concerns mainly caused by the recession, the Hotel Botanico was returning profits and was already internationally renowned.

The old and the new in the Yeoward business came together on 11 April 1979. The Hotel Botanico, which had come about because people had worked together successfully, hosted a dinner to commemorate Manuel Abreu's record of sixty years' service with "Casa Yeoward", another example of the importance of people to the business. During the dinner, to which Abreu was able to bring his mother, then aged ninety-eight, he was presented with a proposal, signed by the entire staff of "Casa Yeoward" and submitted to Madrid, that he should be awarded the *Medalla al Merito en el Trabajo*. Madrid promptly agreed and three weeks later the Minister of Labour made the presentation to Abreu, who added another two years to his service record before retiring.

chapter seven

1979–1989

THE reputation of the Hotel Botanico continued to grow and in the summer of 1980 Tony Yeoward, on behalf of the hotel, received from the Spanish Minister of Tourism in Madrid the distinction of the *Placa de Plata de la Orden del Merito Turistico*. The hotel's entire staff shared in the award a few days later when Tony thanked them all at a celebration for the hard work and effort that had gained the award for the hotel.

The Hotel Botanico also became the first in the Canary Islands to receive the distinction of meriting the maximum official classification of "Five Star Gran Lujo", of which there were only ten hotels throughout the whole of Spain. Thus there were probably many who eyed the international prestige of the Hotel Botanico enviously but it was nevertheless a surprise when Tony received a telephone call in November 1980 from Felix Gallardo's secretary to ask for Tony's agreement and that of his family and Intercon SA for the sale of Gallardo's stake in the hotel. Tony assumed that this was simply a transfer of Gallardo's interest within his own family but was told that this was not the case. The sale was to a third party but Gallardo's secretary refused to tell Tony either the name of the party concerned or the price being paid. More than interested to discover just what was going on, Tony took the next flight to Barcelona the following day so that he could confront Gallardo personally on the matter.

When he met Gallardo in his Barcelona office, Tony was told that Gallardo had supposed he would have no interest in purchasing the stake and he had therefore agreed a price for the whole of his business interests. Gallardo still would not disclose the name of the purchaser but agreed to arrange for Tony to meet representatives of the buyer the following evening. It was only then that Tony discovered that the three men who turned up to meet him were from Spain's largest private holding company, Rumasa, a conglomerate with wide-ranging interests, including hotels. The discussion was polite but cold. Tony expressed his interest in taking up Gallardo's stake but the men from Rumasa told him that it was precisely the shares in the Hotel Botanico which were the most attractive part of the package for them and that as the agreed purchase price was for the whole of Gallardo's business interests, it was not possible to attribute a realistic value to the Hotel Botanico stake alone. If Tony had pressed his case, Rumasa might well have told him that the greater part of the price was for the participation in the hotel – a totally unrealistic valuation. So Rumasa became shareholders in the Hotel Botanico.

Rumasa's involvement in the hotel, through its hotel management subsidiary Hotasa, as well as the undoubted value of the hotel, encouraged a number of the hotel's other shareholders, including Aznar, still in desperate financial straits, to offer their holdings for sale. Hotasa was only too eager to take up these offers. Tony Yeoward, however, was resolute in his determination to purchase for Yeoward as many of the shares offered for sale as he was able, in accordance with the company statutes, although this did place pressure upon financial resources. Two other shareholders also decided to retain their holdings.

Despite initial misgivings, since Rumasa had a dubious business reputation, Hotasa proved itself to be a well-run professional organisation and applied its expertise to advantage in the running of the Hotel Botanico. For example, Hotasa introduced one of Spain's leading luxury hotel managers, Antonio Lopera, who had recently retired, as its professional adviser at the hotel. The Hotasa involvement did lead, however, to the termination on satisfactory terms of the promotional arrangement between the hotel and Brooker since Hotasa had its own established promotional side.

Then in February 1983, while on a visit to the United Kingdom, Tony was listening to the early morning news on his car radio when he heard a shattering announcement. The Spanish Government had expropriated Rumasa "in the national interest", including the entire capital of any other businesses in which Rumasa had an interest. On the night the expropriation took place, the Hotel Botanico, with an unparalleled reputation for quality, was fully booked. It had built up a loyal clientele, including on that night, one couple who were on their twenty-third visit to the hotel in eight years, each stay averaging between two and three weeks' duration.

The claim for compensation which arose from the expropriation occupied most of Tony's time over the next two years. Two separate independent valuations had both reached the same result, and this agreed figure was presented to the Spanish Treasury in Madrid in June 1984. This was not the end of the affair. Many months of arduous and time-consuming negotiations were conducted in Madrid between Tony and the Treasury in an effort to bridge the considerable difference in valuations acceptable to each side. The Treasury was no doubt influenced, in its adherence to a much lower valuation, by the huge public furore developing over the escalating costs of the Rumasa expropriation. A settlement was finally reached only when the Director General himself, who was negotiating on behalf of the Treasury, pointed out that the offer made by the Treasury would be exempt from capital gains taxation, whereas Tony had always believed that any settlement would be subject to normal taxes. This tax exemption brought the Treasury's offer to almost the equivalent level of the higher independent valuation, net of the assumed taxation. The offer was therefore accepted on the basis that the exemption from taxation was enshrined in the final Agreement. The Agreement was duly reworded by the Treasury and the amended version was signed on 13 March 1985. With the payment of the settlement four months later, that appeared to be the end of the matter and an end to the links between Yeoward and the Hotel Botanico.

In that same year Yeoward disposed of its remaining interests in Gran Canaria. The tomato farm at Sardina ran into further trouble when the financial problems of the tenant, Marcelo Baez, became so acute that he was unable to pay the wages of his farmworkers. In an episode reminiscent of the 1930s this, together with the fact that the farm was owned by a foreigner not resident on that island, led to cries for the farm to be taken over by the workforce. The pressure became quite intense and the picketing of the farm aggressive. When Tony Yeoward flew to the island to deal with the situation, he met, alone, several of the union activists in his office, contrary to local advice. This seemed to unsettle the ringleaders, who also discovered that Tony knew more about marketing than they did and that he himself had also been involved in a workers' cooperative. The result was that the unionists left the meeting in agreement with what Tony had told them and intending to raise the necessary funds to purchase the farm themselves. The campaign subsided, the union's attempts to purchase the farm came to nothing and Baez was allowed to remain as tenant until a final solution to the problem had been achieved by Yeoward. This came with the satisfactory sale of the farm in 1985 to a growers' cooperative formed for the purpose and interests in Gran Canaria were finally wound up with the sale of the last of the Sardina building plots.

In Tenerife, the joint management arrangement for the properties owned respectively by Tony Yeoward and the family of the late Bernard Yeoward came to an end in 1982 when Richard Yeoward, Bernard's son, declined to take over the responsibility for the management of his own family properties. The original intentions for the joint development of La Costa farm by Intercon and Bernard not having been realised, and Richard having replaced his father, the basis of the original Agreement needed revision. So it was now agreed that an exchange would be effected whereby Intercon would return its half share in La Costa and would receive two smaller neighbouring farms, Lomo and Rechazos. Tony had doubts about the continued cultivation of bananas on both farms, especially Lomo, but it was nevertheless decided to rework the entire farm, employing considerable numbers of men, and installing an entirely new irrigation system. Lomo improved substantially but the bananas still did not pay.

After several years of expense, the bananas were removed and replaced by raspberries. Tony's first instincts had been correct.

The responsibility for the raspberries was given to Arthur Tabrett, who had been a fruit-grower in Kent and a member of Markads before emigrating to Tenerife. He had been experimenting with the commercial cultivation of various vegetables, especially lettuce, on a small area of Llanos de Mendez which had been cleared of bananas by Tony. This had proved so successful that the two men had agreed to a joint partnership in which Tony provided the land and facilities while Arthur provided his knowledge and expertise. He was an obvious choice to place in charge of the raspberries at Lomo at the end of the 1980s.

It was also in 1982 that Tony was able at last to give his full attention to the continuing development of Yeoward's property interests on Tenerife with the construction of Parque Avoceta, the successor to the completed Edificio Alondra in the El Botanico estate. In connection with the sales of these properties, Intercon employed Brooker as its general sales agent in the United Kingdom and, with Mrs. Mylou Yeoward handling sales on the Island, much closer personal contact with potential clients was achieved.

The reputation and contribution made to the local economy by the Hotel Botanico had been recognised in several ways, most notably when it became the venue for a very distinguished royal visit. King Juan Carlos and Queen Sofia of Spain welcomed to the hotel no less than seven Heads of State who enjoyed a long weekend in its sumptuous surroundings. The Duke and Duchess of Gloucester represented H.M. Queen Elizabeth II and H.R.H. the Duke of Edinburgh, since protocol would not permit them to attend in person because there had never been a royal State visit to Spain by the British monarch – a gap soon to be filled. Also present were Queen Margrethe and Prince Henry of Denmark, Queen Beatrix and Prince Klaus of the Netherlands, King Carl Gustav and Queen Silvia of Sweden, President and Mrs Patrick Hillery of Eire and President and Frau Richard von Weizsacker of West Germany.

It is difficult to conceive where else in the world there could be such a gathering of seven Heads of State in a hotel open to the public, during a period of several days. The occasion was the official inauguration of the International Astrophysical Observatory in the neighbouring island of La Palma, in which all the participating nations were represented. The only accommodation deemed suitable was the Hotel Botanico, with an improvised helicopter landing site across the road, to and from which the guests were driven the 200 metres in closed cars.

The Firm's offices, directly in front of the hotel, were suitably dressed for the occasion, proudly displaying the Union Jack and the Spanish flag alongside each other.

Before the plans had been made for this visit of royalty, the hotel had already taken many bookings for clients. Rather than close the hotel to them, it was agreed that they should be notified in advance, warning them that inevitably they would be subject to certain inconveniences and restrictions of movement during the period, so that they could have the option of either cancelling or transferring to another hotel or arranging a different date. Very few opted to change, anticipating that the excitement would outweigh any inconvenience. In the event, this caused no trouble whatsoever but it did give opportunity to certain light-hearted incidents, such as when a guest in the main hall saw that the King of Spain was coming down the stairs, he hastily fumbled with his camera to take the memorable photograph but to his dismay he could not get the wretched camera to function just when it was most needed. Seeing his predicament, the King walked over to where the guest was standing and, in his perfect English, said "Excuse me, I think it would work better if you were to remove the lens cap first". Whereupon he returned to the stairs to repeat his descent so that the ever-grateful customer could take his shot for posterity!

Naturally there were other amusing incidents. On their second evening, His Majesty invited his guests to go downtown for an impromptu dinner. Not having any transport readily available, he horrified his security officers by marching out to the main road and hailing a passing empty minibus and, when his guests were all aboard, being conscious of the local disappointment of many because of the manner in which all his party were always driven at high speed in closed limousines between the hotel and the helicopter pad, he specifically requested the surprised driver to switch on the interior lights and drive slowly through the popular area of the town "so that we can be seen". When they arrived at the restaurant, they found that it had been hastily cleared of all other guests, an action which cost the chief of security a very severe reprimand later that night when the party had returned to the Hotel Botanico.

Meanwhile, when they had ordered the dinner, there had been momentary consternation when Queen Sofia requested lettuce and it was realised that there was none available. Unbeknown to the diners, an emergency call was made to the Hotel Botanico and within moments the Royal Lettuce was on its way, complete with a police motor-cycle escort.

On Sunday morning the guests were departing and naturally their host was there to wish them farewell. By mid-morning all had gone, except one who was not due to depart until the afternoon. The King was ready for a break. With the Queen near at hand, he wandered casually out of the front door and over to his parked car, where he established conversation with the driver. Within moments, with the keys in his hand, he beckoned to the Queen, who came quickly and jumped into the passenger seat while he got into the driver's seat. Before the security officers realised what was happening they were away, down towards the town where they had last been several years before as

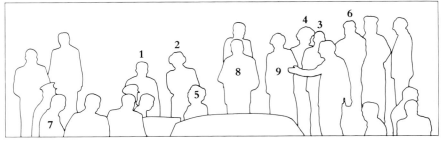

King Juan Carlos and Queen Sofia of Spain with various guests leaving the hotel Botanico during their royal visit, in summer 1985.

1 King Juan Carlos	Spain
2 Queen Sofia	Spain
3 Duke of Gloucester	Great Britain
4 Duchess of Gloucester	Great Britain
5 Queen Beatrix	Netherlands
6 Prince Klaus	Netherlands
7 President Patrick Hillery	Eire
8 President Richard von Weizsäcker	Germany
9 Frau von Weizsäcker	Germany

Opposite: Some of the letters received by Mr. Yeoward from the Royal visitors after their stay at the Botanico, in which they express the pleasant memories they have of Tenerife and in particular, of the Hotel Botanico and area.

1979–1989

Royal Palace, Stockholm, July 12, 1985

Mr. Anthony R. Yeoward
"El Botanico"
Apartado 2
Puerto de la Cruz
Tenerife
Islas Canarias

Dear Mr. Yeoward,

I am asked by Their Majesties The King [...]
to convey to you Their sincere thanks [...]
of July 6, 1985, as well as for the [...]
which Their Majesties will keep as a [...]
stay in the Botanico.

Yours sincerely,

Claes Nordström
Surveyor of the Court

July 16th, 1985

Her Majesty the Queen has asked
me to express to you Her sincere
thanks for your kind letter and
the 2 photographs from the Bota-
nic Hotel.
Yours truly
Alette Bardenfleth
Lady-in-waiting

Royal Netherlands Embassy

Madrid, September 2, 1985

Dear Sir,

At the request of Her Majesty Queen Beatrix I have the
honour to transmit to you Her Majesty's gratitude for the
photographs, forwarded to Her Majesty through this Embassy.

With kind regards,

E.J. Korthals Altes
Ambassador

CASA DE S.M. EL REY
EL SECRETARIO GENERAL
Palacio de la Zarzuela
MADRID, 12 de Julio de 1985

Señor
ANTHONY R. YEOWARD
El Botánico, Apartado 2
PUERTO DE LA CRUZ – TENERIFE

Mi querido amigo:

SU MAJESTAD EL REY me encarga a[...]
carta de 6 del actual, y darle las gracias en Su nomb[...]
tuoso saludo, por las bonitas fotografías que tan am[...]
vía.

Al participárselo, cordialmente [...]

SABINO FERNANDEZ CAMPO

c/j.

BRITISH EMBASSY,
MADRID.

11 July 1985

Anthony R Yeoward Esq
'El Botanico'
Apartado 2
Puerto de la Cruz
Tenerife
Islas Canarias

Dear Mr Yeoward

Many thanks for your letter of 6 July and the photographs
taken when the Duke and Duchess of Gloucester were in
Tenerife. I have sent these to the Duke's Private Secretary,
and I am sure they will be very well received.

Mary and I were so pleased to see you both again. I hope it
will not be too long before we return. Meanwhile all our
best wishes and many thanks again for your letter.

Yours
Lord N Go[...]

BUNDESPRÄSIDIALAMT
Az.: II/1-6626-1709/84

Herrn
Anthony R. Yeoward
"El Botanico"
Puerto de la Cruz
Tenerife / Islas Canarias

Sehr geehrter Herr Yeoward,

der Herr Bundespräsident, de[...]
befindet, hat mich gebeten, [...]
Brief vom 6. Juli 1985 zu da[...]

Das Bild, das Sie zur Erinne[...]
"Botanico" übersandten, hat [...]
enthalt in diesem schönen Ho[...]
pischen Garten anläßlich der [...]
Observatorien bleibt in best[...]

Mit freundlichen Grüßen
Im Auftrag

v. Puttkamer

OIFIG RÚNAÍ AN UACHTARÁIN
OFFICE OF THE SECRETARY TO THE PRESIDENT
BAILE ÁTHA CLIATH 8
DUBLIN

12 Iuil, 1985

Dear Mr. Yeoward,

The President has asked me to thank you for your
letter of 6th July, 1985 and for the photographs which
were enclosed.

He is very pleased to have this Memento of his stay
at the Botanico.

With every good wish,

Yours sincerely,

P. O'Malley
Personal Secretary

Mr. Anthony R. Yeoward

From: Lt. Col. Sir Simon Bland
KCVO

KENSINGTON PALACE
LONDON W8 4PU
TELEPHONE 01-[...]

17 July 1985

Dear Mr Yeoward,

The Duke and Duchess of Gloucester have
asked me to thank you for your letter of
6 July and for the nice photographs you sent.

Their Royal Highnesses were pleased they
were able to meet you and have asked me to say
that the photographs will be a nice memento of
a very enjoyable short stay in Tenerife.

Yours sincerely,
Simon Bland

Anthony R Yeoward Esq

127

Prince and Princess. He remembered the road but what he did not know was that since he was last there it had been made one-way out of town. It is not recorded what the other driver said when, correctly driving out of town, he found himself confronted by a large Mercedes Benz bearing a royal crown in place of a number plate!

Following the royal visit, personal letters were received by Tony from the households of each of the Heads of State, recording their personal appreciation of the Hotel Botanico.

The tradition, reputation and continuing contribution of the Yeoward family itself to the Islands was further recognised by a unique event in October 1988. For the occasion of the first ever royal State visit to Spain by a reigning British monarch, Her Majesty Queen Elizabeth II, accompanied by His Royal Highness the Prince Philip, Duke of Edinburgh, had commanded her ambassador to invite a number of her loyal subjects resident throughout Spain to be presented to her in the Palacio de El Pardo in Madrid. Inevitably the numbers were very restricted – scarcely more than a hundred and most of those invited were active or retired officials of the Consular Corps or of the Anglican Church. Of the select few not falling into either of these categories were Mr. and Mrs. Anthony R. Yeoward, the only members of the entire active business community in Tenerife to be so honoured.

The Palacio de El Pardo, situated just a few miles north west of the city, is an unusually charming palace. More reminiscent of a very well-kept and comfortable hunting lodge set in its own gardens and with an air of homeliness about it, the palace is in complete contrast to the more usual awe-inspiring impressiveness of a royal palace. As the guests arrived from the embassy where they had assembled, the Royal Standard was flying over the main entrance to the palace. With the evening sun sinking behind the hills and the strains of the lone bugle calling from some distant corner of the gardens, the Royal Standard was ceremoniously lowered.

Her Majesty the Queen was radiant and relaxed, wearing an attractive turquoise dress with pearl necklace and pearl and diamond brooch but hatless in the relative informality of a private cocktail party amongst her own subjects – contrasting with the formality of the State functions which were occupying the rest of her time. She demonstrated a keen interest in all that affected her subjects living in Spain, spending almost a whole hour chatting informally with her guests. Those few who had the honour to be present on such an occasion, seeing her so relaxed, so natural, so human, could not fail to be impressed and to feel the greatest admiration for such a gracious lady.

During this period there had also been changes in the British business. The main board had been strengthened in 1979 by the addition of Ron Gill and David Bishop. Ron, who became the Company's Financial Director, had

1979–1989

Ron Gill and David Bishop following their appointment to the Board of Yeoward Brothers Ltd. in Liverpool in 1979.

joined the Firm as an office boy in 1943 and worked his way up through the organisation. David had entered Yeoward Brothers Ltd. as a young man in 1964 and had obtained considerable expertise in shipping during that time. He was now in charge of the Company's shipping operations.

The difficult economic climate in Britain in the late 1970s and early 1980s had an impact on the Company as it did upon many other British businesses. Geoff Jones described this period as "unsettled" and in 1981 wrote that it had been decided "to review fully the Company's activities and to minimise our staff requirements". In 1982, for the first time since the Profit Sharing Scheme had been introduced in 1969, there was no payout as the Company passed its dividend payment.

Then at this difficult time came a terrible blow to the business. Geoff Jones, whose contribution to the produce trade had just been recognised by his appointment as National President of the National Federation of Fruit and Potato Trades and as President of the National Institute of Fresh Produce, had spent a fortnight in January 1983 in the Canary Islands. In early February, on his return to the United Kingdom, he had heard the news of the death of George Simpson and had attended his funeral before returning to Liverpool. He felt unwell at the weekend and did not go to the office on the Monday morning. Soon after noon he was dead.

Geoff had been the linchpin in the management of the British business and while Tony Yeoward recognised that as a consequence he would have to make more frequent visits to Liverpool in the immediate future, it was not possible for him to take over the responsibility for the day-to-day management of the operations. With an eye to the future development of the business, it was agreed that David Bishop should be appointed Managing Director. David was still only thirty-five years old and the only Board member on the right side of his fiftieth birthday.

An additional move, coinciding with the ninetieth anniversary of the founding of the Firm, was the appointment in January 1984 of two non-executive directors to the Board. The first was Keppel Simpson, the son of George Simpson, whose wide-ranging business expertise has since proved more than valuable to Yeoward Brothers Ltd. The second was Rosemary Yeoward, Tony's eldest daughter, who was then working for Peat Marwick Mitchell in Paris and who represented the entry of the family's fourth generation into the Company. Her younger sister, Virginia, joined the Company for three months later that year for work experience before entering university.

In 1985 when the lease on the premises of Old Hall Street, Liverpool ran out, the Company obtained freehold premises in Trueman Street. These had originally been part of the head offices of Threlfalls, an old, independent Liverpool brewery which had been bought by the Whitbread Group and rationalised into the larger organisation. That part of the building purchased by the Company then became Yeoward House and it contained the disused but impressive mahogany-panelled board room which Yeoward would eventually renovate to its former glory.

The fruit business had not had a happy time during the 1980s. The London business had made losses in the early 1980s but the Liverpool branch had been reopened in an attempt to complement and enhance the existing London operations. When the decision was finally made to close the London branch in 1988 after further losses, it was also decided to close the Liverpool branch. With Liverpool as the only remaining part of Yeoward's once-extensive fruit business, there seemed little reason for maintaining it, especially since the volatility of the seasonal fruit trade posed such a potential threat to the financial stability of the UK business that Tony was no longer prepared to continue with it. The Liverpool premises were eventually sold in 1988 but even then it was discovered that a considerable volume of stock had vanished, creating a branch loss of more than a hundred thousand pounds for the final year.

The demise of the fruit business, one of the original two business of Yeoward Brothers, was an unhappy experience but Shipping, the other original part of the business, had fared much better under the direction of David Bishop. The outlook had not been good in 1979 after the final collapse of Aznar had left Yeoward bereft of any shipping links. The period between 1979 and 1982 was generally in limbo. Yeoward had attempted for one summer season to run a chartered vessel carrying export cargo only, in conjunction with a German-owned Spanish firm, Erhardt. The intention was that this service would maintain a Yeoward presence in the trade to enable Yeoward to become involved in the winter fruit trade when the contracts were let again, but the service could not be sustained because it lost too much money. Yeoward also approached Frucasa, who had taken over the Canary fruit run to Liverpool from Aznar, to act as their agent in Liverpool, but to no avail.

The Company's long-established and respected reputation within the Canary fruit trade, however, was instrumental in an unexpected revival in Yeoward's shipping fortunes. In September 1982 a representative of the Canary Islands growers and exporters contacted David Bishop, by now the sole shipping employee within Yeoward, and asked him if Yeoward could handle Nissui Line vessels bringing Canary fruit into Liverpool the following month. Without hesitation David accepted the challenge, recruited staff, and brought back from retirement one experienced former employee, Vic Parry. The operation was handled with such success that Yeoward have continued to act as the agent for Nissui Shipping Corporation's Canary fruit vessels since that time. By 1986, every Monday morning between November and April, the *North Wind* or the *West Wind* alternately arrived in Liverpool to discharge Canary fruit before setting sail once more the same evening. During the 1986 season Yeoward Brothers Ltd. were instrumental in supplying three million cases of Canary tomatoes in the United Kingdom as well as quantities of cucumbers and peppers.

A major change brought about by this relationship came in 1987 when the Yeoward shipping activity moved with Nissui from Liverpool to Southampton. The principal reason for this was the desire of the exporters, the importers and the supermarkets (who were the main purchasers of Canary fruit) to concentrate their operations in the south of England. This began in a small way with four vessels into Southampton during the season but has grown considerably over the ensuing years. The main difficulty was and has remained the lack of any shipping business outside the traditional winter fruit season although Yeoward has tried hard to extend this seasonal base. Nevertheless, the efforts of David Bishop and his team during the 1980s had established once more a strong Yeoward presence in the shipping world which had seemed remote at the outset.

The withdrawal of Yeoward from fruit had been foreseen in the review of the business conducted after the death of Geoff Jones. In its place, it had been decided that the Company would continue to develop its travel interests. With that in mind, an 85% stake in a small chain of travel agencies in Liverpool, Autopass Agencies, was purchased in 1983. In conjunction with the continued involvement of Autopass's founders, Terry and Brian Hughes, and with Yeoward's own Griffin Travel operation, it was intended to establish a chain of ten to a dozen agencies throughout Liverpool.

It was while pursuing other possible acquisitions in the travel world that the Company was advised by its auditors of an opportunity to invest in a completely different but profitable business. An edible oil transport business had been built up by a family in Birkenhead and had been very successful but had stumbled when it had lost a relatively major customer. This was not critical to the future of the business but when the Company's bank was informed, it panicked and sent in the receiver. There was no doubt at all that the company had a bright future and, assured of this, Tony Yeoward agreed that Yeoward should seek to obtain a stake in it. The result was that Yeoward Brothers Ltd., through a newly-formed subsidiary, Yeoward Brothers (Tankers) Ltd., obtained a 51% holding, the remaining 49% being retained by the original family who continued to be responsible for the day-to-day running of the business. It soon became obvious that in such a capital-intensive field the new business was under-capitalised and therefore, with the aid of loans from Yeoward and the subscription of additional capital in identical proportions, the tanker fleet was overhauled and expanded.

The resurgence of the shipping business, the expansion of the travel business and the management time required to be spent upon the new tanker business all added up to a considerable strain upon the limited management resources available at Yeoward Brothers Ltd. While this was alleviated by improved financial reporting systems and the introduction of regular quarterly Board meetings, it was obvious that the extent of Yeoward's business by the late 1980s was more than could be assimilated by the Company's existing senior executives. David Bishop's shipping expertise was essential to the continued success of the Yeoward shipping operations, still the cornerstone of the British business, and Ron Gill was fully occupied in exercising vigilant financial control over the travel agencies and the tanker business, whose daily management still remained with their founders. With that and the future development of the Group in mind, it was unanimously agreed at a Board meeting in 1989 that the Yeoward Group, as it was now known, should recruit an experienced chief executive to attend to the overall management of the Group's businesses. The specific brief which Tony Yeoward handed to the recruitment consultant was that the ideal candidate should be aged in his late forties, with considerable management expertise, probably with an accounting background, experienced in running a number of subsidiaries and preferably with antecedents in the North West. His remit would be to review the Group's activities with the objective of achieving an acceptable and stable level of profitability, sufficient to sustain the Group for the foreseeable future. It was accepted that changes might be necessary and further acquisitions might be appropriate but the long-term objective was financial stability. In mid-1989 Malcolm Holt joined Yeoward as its first Group Chief Executive.

chapter eight

1989 and Onward

MALCOLM Holt came to the Yeoward Group with considerable management experience. He had trained as an accountant before entering general management in 1970 and had subsequently managed companies in differing industries before progressing to divisional management. He had latterly and for several years been the head of a division of thirteen companies with a turnover of some seventy-five million pounds within a multinational organisation. But there he found that the balance between profit and people had tipped too much in the direction of profit and at the expense of capable staff. The very thing that attracted him to Yeoward was the Company's belief, which stemmed from its tradition as a long-established, family-owned and family-managed company, that committed, capable people were vital to any business because it was only through people that profits were ultimately created.

Malcolm's appointment enabled Tony Yeoward to concentrate once again upon Yeoward's Canary interests. In the Islands, the decision was taken to postpone further property development because of the uncertain economic outlook. Instead, in association with Arthur Tabrett, Tony decided to experiment with the cultivation of raspberries on the Lomo farm. Previous experiments by others on the Islands had failed, yet within a year Arthur Tabrett had found a variety of raspberry which could be grown in the Islands with success. As a result of this, the whole farm was prepared for raspberry cultivation and some 35,000 plants were imported from the United Kingdom. Although there was some uncertainty about local markets because the fruit was relatively unknown, a successful export market to London was developed with some five tons of fruit being shipped there during 1990 - 1991. During the latter year irrigation problems resulted in the loss of half the crop but they were overcome and the fruit was sold with success locally. This was fortunate since by late 1991 London prices had dropped substantially and very little fruit was then exported. Arthur Tabrett subsequently returned to the United Kingdom at the end of the 1991 season and the farm has since been run by "Casa Yeoward" alone with continuing success.

By now, the original concept of the residential garden estate of Parque Avoceta in El Botanico had reached completion. Consisting exclusively of luxurious residential dwellings, in several buildings, none of which was more than four floors in height, the development is surrounded by beautiful gardens which have been universally praised by all who have seen them. The five million pound investment had been constructed in phases and very selectively marketed through R. M. Brooker Ltd., with great emphasis being placed by Tony Yeoward and his wife on their personal relationships with the clients, thus achieving an unusually harmonious and friendly community.

During almost a quarter of a century Tony had observed how dwellings which Intercon had built and sold had substantially increased in value as it became widely recognised that El Botanico was the most desirable neighbourhood in which to live. But he had also observed another phenomenon which initially had surprised him. His customers had been typically in their sixties and had been delighted with their homes where they could enjoy their retirement. But when the time came for the property to pass to their heirs, it was sometimes looked upon by its inheritor as a nuisance, because of the trouble to arrange its sale from abroad, despite the very substantial gains realised in the capital value. Coincident to this latter observation and during the early stages of the development of Parque Avoceta, an amendment was introduced to the law governing the renting of residential property in Spain. Up to this point, residential letting had virtually ceased due to the practical impossibility of being able to recover possession of the property at the termination of the agreed period. The combination of these two factors provided the opportunity for Tony to offer a form of leasehold arrangement whereby the client could enjoy the full use of the property for an agreed period as if it was owned by him. He could also avoid the potential inconveniences for the next generation, and perhaps more importantly, avoid tying up to so much capital in the property. Initially, this arrangement was offered for a specific number of years but the introduction of computerisation enabled infinite flexibility to be introduced in order to tailor the agreement to suit each individual client's circumstances, even to the extent of lifetime leaseholds. Obviously such an arrangement could only be offered by a promotor who had absolute faith in the future value of the property and thus it was found that the offer of the alternative of either freehold or leasehold not only broadened the attraction to the customer but even reassured the potential freehold purchaser. And in all of this time Tony and his wife maintained their absolute opposition to the introduction of any form of "time-share", so totally discredited in Spain.

Not surprisingly, the temporary down-turn in the international property market in the early 1990s affected Parque Avoceta. But with its now mature gardens and in contrast to others, it is emerging from the economic recession in a healthy condition and able to offer a more attractive proposition than ever before. This stability has been brought about mainly through the conservative manner in which the development was constructed in phases, thus avoiding heavy burdens of indebtedness and the consequent continuous pressure for sales. It has also benefited from the excellent reputation it has earned since conception, to the point where present clients are now the Company's most effective sales ambassadors.

A more time-consuming concern, which still continues to occupy a substantial proportion of Tony Yeoward's attention, was the attempt by the Spanish Government in 1992 to charge Yeoward with taxation on the nett compensation paid back to Yeoward in 1985 by the Spanish treasury for the expropriation of Yeoward's stake in the Hotel Botanico. This was despite the fact that in the negotiations, this sum, reduced to approximately half of the independent professional valuation, had been specifically declared nett of taxation by the Director General in the Treasury Ministry in Madrid and that exemption had been encapsulated in the Agreement drafted by the same Treasury Ministry and signed at that time in the name of the Spanish State.

Naturally this new claim, condemned by all those who have knowledge of the extraordinary case, is being strongly contested. Before the dispute can pass to the Courts of Justice in Spain and if necessary the International Courts, it first had to be considered by a Tribunal operated directly under the control of the Treasury Ministry. After rather more than a year, this "Tribunal" has produced a remarkable ruling, amounting to an accusation against their own Directorate General. Meanwhile, with future local investment and employment suffering, to the detriment of the Spanish economy, Yeoward is left in the midst of this cross-fire, finding itself obliged to bear the burden of time and expense to safeguard its legitimate interests.

Back in the United Kingdom, before Yeoward's new Chief Executive made proposals to the rest of the Board, he took stock of the Group. Malcolm Holt found a shipping business which was at the core of the Group's activities and performing well. But, like David Bishop, he saw that concerted efforts must be made to extend the Group's shipping activities beyond the Canary fruit season. The travel business was more problematical, with optimistic assumptions being made about results, too much emphasis upon sales as opposed to profits and a need to bring all the travel businesses under a single banner. The trading title of "Mersey Travelworld" was subsequently introduced for all branches in 1990.

At this time in 1989 the tanker business was a prosperous part of the Group but it was one which was very difficult to control because of the founding family's large minority shareholding and their dominance over its daily operations. While Malcolm felt the business had growth potential, he also believed strongly that the tanker business should adopt the operating and management reporting policies laid down by Yeoward as the majority shareholder.

The summary of Malcolm's first report to the Board made in October 1989 crystallised the problem and spelt out that, while improvements could be made to the Group's existing businesses, in order to justify a continuing head office operation in Liverpool which he regarded as fundamental to the identity of the Group, it was essential that new profit-earning opportunities were sought out and vigorously pursued.

It was therefore quite clear that the first phase in the new direction to be taken by the Group was to resolve the problems in its existing businesses. Shipping continued to manage its Canary fruit operations effectively, although its pursuit of other sources of business met with little success, but it was the Group's tanker and travel businesses which were proving troublesome.

Neither Yeoward nor the founding family were happy with the existing arrangements at the tanker company. Yeoward knew little of what was going on at the business and was unable to construct and implement any development plans while the family regarded the day-to-day management of the business as their concern alone. These problems were highlighted when the family refused to co-operate with Yeoward's proposal to hire external professional consultants in order to prepare a marketing plan aimed at consolidating the tankers' UK market position and exploiting opportunities in Europe. The Group felt this project was vital in view of the risks and opportunities that would arise from the new European "Open Market" legislation due to be introduced in 1992 which would trigger the easing of trade barriers throughout the EC. The crunch eventually came, however, when Yeoward's attempt to put in place new budgetary controls and management reporting met with resistance from the family. In a clearly untenable position, and after weeks of argument and discussion, the Yeoward Board, on Malcolm's recommendation, decided to dispose of their stake in the tanker business and, conveniently coinciding with this decision, an offer was received from the family to purchase the Yeoward shareholding. After amicable negotiations, Yeoward sold its stake back to them for a very acceptable price in early 1990.

While the sale of the tanker business had removed a difficult operational situation which had been absorbing considerable management time, it had also removed one of the Group's valuable sources of profit. Thus the need to find replacement profit-earners was emphasised not only to provide necessary income for the Group but also to further Tony Yeoward's vision for the development of the Group.

Malcolm Holt thus recommended to his fellow directors that three related steps should be taken. Firstly, the Group should seek to acquire new profitable businesses. In particular, distribution was identified as an industry sector which complemented the remaining Yeoward Group activities. As a service activity, it was in tune with the culture of the Group and as a widely based industry, where the same approach applied to a variety of goods, the opportunities would be greater. Malcolm Holt felt that there were two types of company which would be attractive to Yeoward. These were the family-owned business whose owners were seeking to retire and dispose of the business and the successful company which had outgrown its entrepreneurial founder and required additional capital and expertise to develop further. The Yeoward Board accepted these recommendations and in a clear demonstration of its commitment to the future, the Yeoward family proposed and implemented a reconstruction of the Company's share capital, resulting in the injection of substantial new funds to support the agreed strategies.

It was a local company, a distributor of industrial safety products, industrial consumables and medical products, which first attracted the attention of Malcolm Holt and his colleagues. E. & L. Sorsky Ltd. was a long-established and profitable family business, founded in 1919, whose owners, without any family successors, were seeking retirement. Successful negotiations were concluded in late 1990 and Sorsky became a wholly owned subsidiary of the Yeoward Group. Part of the purchase price was based upon a multiple of the first year's profits but the owners of the business were so confident that Sorsky would make these profits under Yeoward's control that they declined to stay with the business for longer than six months after the sale had been agreed, preferring instead to activate their retirement plans as early as possible. Upon their departure and in line with long-standing Yeoward practice, Malcolm Holt appointed new operational management from within the company and in the first year the business out-performed expectations, thus providing a bonus on the expected sale price for the previous owners. Under Yeoward's control, Sorsky has continued to grow healthier each year despite the deep recession and has expanded both its scale of operations geographically and its range of products.

Malcolm's second recommendation was that the shipping business should be expanded. There was a generally agreed desire to build up the Yeoward presence in Liverpool once again as well as to expand the business beyond the limited Canary fruit season. A consultant was therefore retained to identify appropriate shipping-related businesses for possible acquisition. He quickly found and recommended to Yeoward two privately-owned deep-sea freight-forwarding businesses, Haywood Shipping Ltd. and H. H. Hughes Shipping Ltd. Yeoward bought both businesses in late 1991 and they were transferred to Yeoward's Liverpool head office under the management of David Bishop. Both businesses returned the expected profits in their first year and the Group attempted to repeat this success with the acquisition of a further similar business, G. A. Shipping Ltd. in 1992. This latter purchase has so far only had modest success but in March 1993 all these activities were brought under the new banner of Yeoward Shipping Services and placed in the charge of a newly appointed forwarding manager, whose brief is to expand this fledgling side of the shipping division under David Bishop's guidance. A further encouraging development in Liverpool in mid-1993 was the appointment of Yeoward as the agent for an international shipping company based in the south of England. This move has enhanced Yeoward's presence at the Liverpool Docks where they supervise all requirements for regular Esso tankers and "break-bulk" multi-purpose vessels from South America.

The Southampton operations, in the meantime, had been consistently successful, with Yeoward providing a comprehensive agency service for each vessel from the Canaries to Southampton. During the twenty-six week season from November to April, Yeoward handles one vessel each week. The voyage from the Canaries takes five days and the small team in Southampton, overseen by David Bishop in Liverpool, is kept busy monitoring the offloading of pallets of fruit totalling over 2,000 in a typical week. Yeoward also handles all shipping related matters, from pilots and tugs to manning and stores, as well as ensuring that the vessel is turned around speedily. It checks cargo quantities, the quality of the handling (in order to ensure that any claims can be properly settled), and ensures cargoes are correctly discharged and delivered to the right importer.

With its historical involvement and experience, Yeoward's depth of knowledge of the Canary fruit trade makes it more like an owner's supervisor than just an agent. The shipping staff liaise between the stevedores and the fruit-importers and provide the importers with detailed information about the vessel's voyage, including the time of arrival and length of discharge – so vital in the handling of fresh fruit. The effectiveness of this entire exercise and the efficiency of the discharge and onward despatch operations are demonstrated weekly with over 60% of each vessel's produce being on sale in retail stores throughout the UK within twelve hours of the discharge being completed. Although strictly speaking Yeoward's responsibilities end once the cargo has been loaded onto importers' transportation, the Southampton staff maintain a close interest in the ensuing stages before delivery occurs because of their longstanding working relationship with their customers.

But there is still that seasonal gap at Southampton which remains to be plugged. Yeoward's particular strengths are strangely also a disadvantage in seeking more general out-of-season shipping business in that they are so

1989 and onward

Left: Mr. Anthony R. Yeoward, present Chairman of the Yeoward Group of Companies.

Bottom: Tony and Mylou Yeoward on the occasion of their presentation to Her Majesty Queen Elizabeth II on her royal State Visit to Spain – October 1988.

Bottom Left: Tomatoes being unloaded at Southampton from Nissui ships – late 1980s.

Right: Tanker rig – late 1980s.

Below: Yeoward's fruit activities at Southampton – late 1980s.

Below right: Fruit distribution trailer – late 1980s.

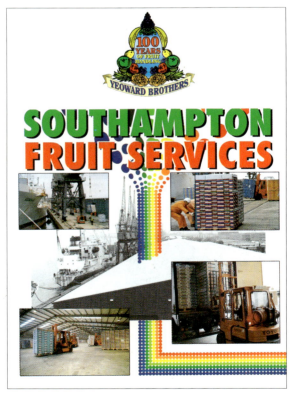

1989 and onward

Top: Parque Avoceta – 1993.

Left: Mature gardens of Hotel Botanico, 1993 – less than 20 years after planting.

Right: The Board of Directors of Yeoward Group of Companies, December 1993. Left to right: David Bishop; Brian Adams *(Company Secretary);* Malcolm Holt; Tony Yeoward; Keppel Simpson; Rosemary Chatin *(née Yeoward);* Ron Gill.

Below right: The refurbished Yeoward Board Room, Yeoward House, Liverpool 1993.

closely identified with the Canary fruit trade. It is also difficult to break into existing year-round shipping agency service because of strong links between shipping lines and their agents which have usually been established for many years. Nevertheless, the search will continue and Yeoward's chances of finding such business must increase with every further year of successful operation at Southampton.

The third recommendation Malcolm had made to his Board colleagues, after the sale of the shares in the tanker business, was that a critical review of the future viability of the travel division should be carried out.

The halcyon days which the travel business and indeed the whole travel industry had enjoyed in the early 1980s had been replaced by much more intense competition as the decade wore on. Despite this developing situation, in early 1990 Yeoward had been persuaded to add to their travel network a single small travel agency in Birkenhead, which they were able to buy at an advantageous price. This was at the behest of Terry Hughes, the enthusiastic Managing Director of the travel division, who reasoned that it offered the prospect of good returns once it had been integrated into the more modern approach of the Yeoward division and its additional volume would assist Yeoward in negotiating better rebates with the tour operators. Another reason for its purchase was that it added to the geographical spread of the small Yeoward travel division, giving it better balance as its first branch on the other side of the Mersey. Certainly, some of these expected benefits were achieved but, although the management was strengthened and operational changes introduced, the new branch fell short of the anticipated profits as the climate in the trade became more and more competitive.

Then, in late 1990, the flagship travel branch in Huyton, located in a busy shopping centre and without any close competitors, lost 40% of its turnover in a single season when a national chain opened a branch nearby. All these factors, but particularly the crushing competition from the large national chains, saw Yeoward's travel business slump from profit to loss in the space of three years between 1989 and 1991.

By 1991, when Tony's youngest daughter Virginia, having recently graduated in Business Studies, joined Malcolm Holt as his Personal Assistant with particular involvement in the travel division, the whole division was struggling in a much tougher environment. There were no management communication problems – the relationship between Yeoward's Head Office and the managers of its travel businesses was harmonious – it was simply that Yeoward found itself caught in a cleft stick. A retail travel business, with its high operating costs and low gross margins, demands high volume throughput and it had become apparent that to succeed in travel one either had to offer a very personal individual service, as typified by the specialist individual travel agent, or belong to a large multiple chain, strong enough to bargain with tour operators and thus able to offer client discounts in the competition for volume business. Neither of these options, however, applied to Yeoward's travel business. It possessed only seven branches, yet it was not a homogeneous business so it could not offer personalised service similar to an owner/proprietor-managed outlet. At the same time, the business was faced with the discounts being offered by aggressive national chains. Therefore, this difficult situation provided a choice of either losing margins through discounting in the hope that volumes would increase, or not discounting and hoping to retain sufficient volume to survive. Not surprisingly Yeoward, in common with many other smaller travel agents, found this position untenable.

In late 1991, therefore, again on the advice of Malcolm Holt, the Yeoward Board decided that the travel division should be sold if possible or closed down if not. Closure would have been very costly so it was with some satisfaction that the business, and the employment it gave, was sold to a local company in early 1992.

Malcolm continued to seek new businesses, particularly to add to the shipping and new distribution divisions, but this was without success until an unusual introduction by the Group's bankers resulted in the next acquisition. This was a Dundee-based service business established and successfully operated by a man and wife team who wished to retire upon the sale of the company. J. Jupp and Co. Ltd. was the largest saw-sharpening firm in Scotland, servicing a wide range of industries, from engineering to paper mills, and it was also a major supplier of band saws and circular saws. Apart from it being a suitable "fit" with existing Group operations, Malcolm Holt and Tony Yeoward were attracted by the value of the company's assets, its current profitability and its prospects for further growth. It was also recognised that Dundee could be a second strategic location for extending Sorsky's operations into Scotland. Jupp was subsequently acquired and became a wholly owned subsidiary of the Yeoward Group in April 1993.

Yeoward has benefited greatly from its recent acquisitions and will continue to do so. Together with the remaining, traditional businesses, they have combined to fulfil the first stage of the restructuring plans established by Malcolm Holt and Tony Yeoward in 1989. The Group now rests once more on solid foundations which will be developed organically in a professional and controlled manner and be complemented by new businesses brought in as appropriate opportunities arise. Thus, as the Company approaches the culmination of its first hundred years and with stability now firmly re-established, it is once again facing an exciting future. There is in place an equally restructured executive management team headed by Malcolm Holt, which possesses all the modern, professional management skills and combines these with long experience of the traditional operations for so long a part of Yeoward history and an equally essential part of its future. There is once more a great optimism within the Group that the combination of all these factors will ensure that the future is a particularly bright, healthy and successful one.

In managing the Group from Yeoward's Head Office, Malcolm is ably supported by a strong Board of fellow directors, although Virginia Yeoward left the Group in August 1992 and moved to London. Virginia's elder sister, Rosemary, however, continues as a non-executive Group director, representing the fourth generation of the Yeoward family involved in the Company. Ron Gill retired in 1992 but, with his wealth of experience, also remains on the Board as a non-executive director. Brian Adams was appointed in his place as Company Secretary and Group Financial Controller. David Bishop knows everything there is to know about the shipping business and is steeped in the management philosophy of the Yeoward Group. Keppel Simpson, as an ex-director of P. A. Management Consultants and now a prominent consultant in his own right, brings his breadth of business experience to the Board as a non-executive director. His long-standing friendship with Tony Yeoward and his family's part in the Firm's history, provide an understanding of the Group ethos which would be impossible to replace. With this team, under the chairmanship of Tony Yeoward, the Yeoward Group is more than capable of expanding successfully both organically through its existing interests and also through the acquisition of others. But above all, the fact that the Yeoward name continues into its second century is a testament to the farsightedness, determination and vision of Tony Yeoward, whose respect for the Yeoward tradition built up by his father and his grandfather has refused to let him do otherwise.

Epilogue

So, as ever, history continues to repeat itself. As
YEOWARD BROTHERS LTD.
proudly approaches its centenary, it would not be amiss to read again the description of how it all began:

> ... the national and world economy had been going through a severe depression, with several financial crises and only brief periods of relative calm; therefore the general outlook on the part of businessmen at that period was one of pessimism and fear of even worse to come.

This referred to the general situation in the early 1890s. A century later, describing the early 1990s, it is unlikely that one would wish to change a single word.

If it perhaps appears that after a hundred years nothing much has changed at Yeoward, how does one explain what has been achieved in all this time? Naturally, all the original participants have long since departed. People have come and people have gone but at the turn of the century the Firm of YEOWARD BROTHERS has outlived them all, and now stands ready to face the challenges of its second century.

In trying to assess what has given it this power of longevity, it is clear that it is not any ability to avoid mistakes! Many have been made, and unfortunately, many have been repeated since human beings sometimes omit to learn from history or to learn to avoid mistakes which were invented long before. There have been occasions when the very existence of the Firm has been in the gravest of danger and equally there have been many occasions when it has "bucked the trend". Indeed, at this very cycle of general malaise and economic difficulty, the prospects for the Company have not looked brighter for many years; its fortunes are rising as the tide ebbs.

Perhaps the answer to this conundrum of longevity truly lies in just two words:

Honesty and Humanity

Those who have been honoured to follow in his footsteps have constantly endeavoured to emulate the high example which Richard Yeoward established at the outset. He always held fast to two basic principles; firstly that no matter how difficult the existing circumstances,

Honesty must prevail

and secondly, but of equal importance, that while without profits sooner or later there is no business, to everybody's loss, it should never be forgotten that

Business is People.

No business can exist successfully if its principal component – human beings – is forgotten or ignored. We all have our failings and our weaknesses – and our strengths.

PERSEVERA PER SEVERA!

ONWARD TO THE SECOND CENTURY!

TONY YEOWARD (December 1993)

appendix

Yeoward Line

Fleet List

Name : **AVOCET**
Type : Steel screw steam ship 209 h.p.
Acquired : 1900
Gross Tons : 1408
Built : 1885 – Caledon Shipbuilders, Dundee
Remarks : Bought from Cork Steam Ship Company Ltd. Sunk by submarine 19 April 1917.

Name : **ARDEOLA**
Type : Steel screw steam ship 194 h.p.
Acquired : 1901
Gross Tons : 1204
Built : 1888 – Caledon Shipbuilders, Dundee
Remarks : Formally the *Fulmar*. Bought from Cork Steam Ship Company Ltd. Sunk in collision 10 December 1903.

Name : **AVETORO**
Type : Steel screw steam ship 194 h.p.
Acquired : 1903
Gross Tons : 1234
Built : 1890 – Caledon Shipbuilders, Dundee
Remarks : Formerly the *Egret*. Bought from Cork Steam Ship Company Ltd. Missing presumed lost by enemy action in November 1915.

Name : **ALCA**
Type : Steel screw steam auxiliary ketch 4 h.p.
Acquired : 1904
Gross Tons : 194
Built : 1898 – Tonning, Germany
Remarks : Formerly the *Stefanie*. Bought from Heyne & Hessenmuller, Hamburg, for the inter-island service. Sold in 1916 to a Spanish shipowner in Bilbao and renamed *Laida*. Sank off Requejada (near Bilbao) on 8 February 1941.

Name : **ARDEOLA**
Type : Steel screw steam ship 234 h.p.
Gross Tons : 1414
Built : 1904 for Yeoward – Caledon Shipbuilders, Dundee
Remarks : Sold in 1911 to the St Lawrence Steam Ship Company Ltd. Renamed the *Marwenna*, and sunk by submarine in May 1915.

Name : **AGUILA**
Type : Steel screw steam ship 278 h.p.
Gross Tons : 2114
Built : 1909 for Yeoward – Caledon Shipbuilders, Dundee
Remarks : Sunk by submarine in March 1915.

Name : **ANDORINHA**
Type : Steel screw steam ship 207 h.p.
Gross Tons : 2548
Built : 1911 for Yeoward – Caledon Shipbuilders, Dundee
Remarks : Sold in 1930 to the Pacific Steam Navigation Company Ltd. and renamed *Chaperico*. Sold in 1934, renamed *Vina del Mar*, no longer registered 1965.

Name : **ARDEOLA**
Type : Steel screw steam ship 207 h.p.
Gross Tons : 3139
Built : 1912 for Yeoward – Caledon Shipbuilders, Dundee
Remarks : Captured November 1942, renamed *Aderno* and sunk by Allied forces in July 1943.

Name : **ALONDRA**
Type : Steel screw steam ship 380 h.p.
Acquired : 1915
Gross Tons : 2244
Built : 1899 – D. J. Dunlop & Co., Glasgow
Remarks : Formerly the *Don Hugo*. Bought from Rio Tinto Company and wrecked in December 1916.

Name : **AVETORO**
Type : Steam ship
Acquired : 1916
Gross Tons : 2233
Built : 1914
Remarks : Formerly the *Valdes*. Bought from Robert MacAndrew & Co. Ltd. and sunk by submarine on 17 February 1917.

appendix

Name : **AGUILA**
Type : Steel screw steam ship 395 h.p.
Gross Tons : 3255
Built : 1917 for Yeoward – Caledon Shipbuilders, Dundee
Remarks : Sunk by submarine 19 August 1941.

Name : **ALONDRA**
Type : Steel screw steam ship 300 h.p.
Gross Tons : 3445
Built : 1922 for Yeoward – Caledon Shipbuilders, Dundee
Remarks : Sold in 1938 to Chilean State Railways and broken up in 1961.

Name : **AVOCETA**
Type : Steel screw steam ship 300 h.p.
Gross Tons : 3442
Built : 1923 for Yeoward – Caledon Shipbuilders, Dundee
Remarks : Sunk by submarine 25 September 1941.

Name : **ALCA**
Type : Steel screw steam ship 300 h.p.
Gross Tons : 3712
Built : 1927 for Yeoward – Caledon Shipbuilders, Dundee
Remarks : Broken up in 1955.

sunward by yeoward

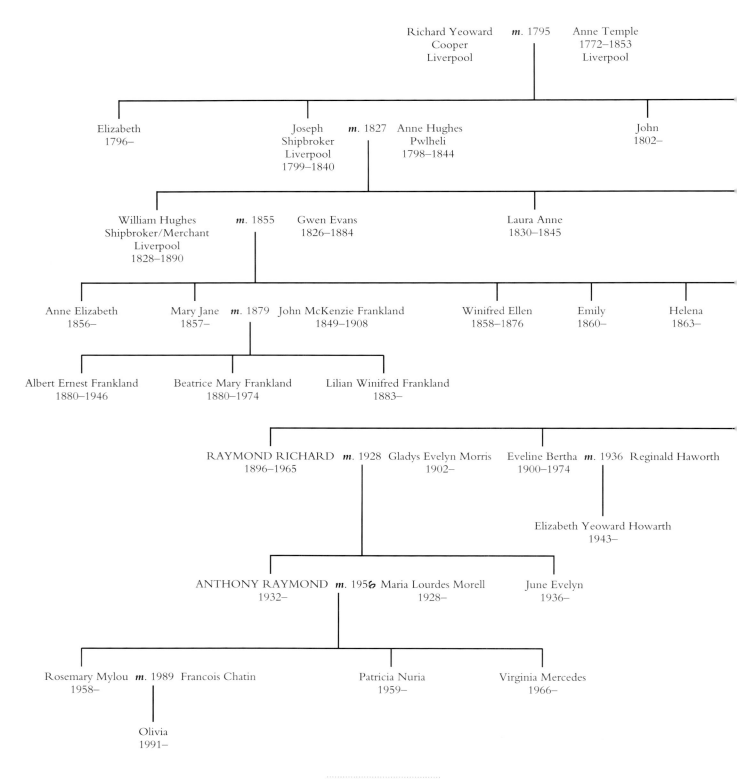

family tree

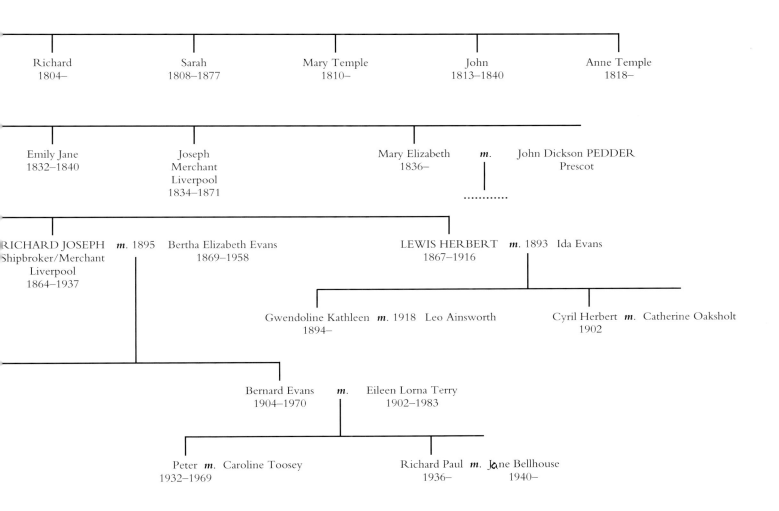

151

Index

Page numbers in *italic* type are references to illustrations

Abreu, Manuel 64-66, 111, 120
Adams, Brian *142*, 145
Aguilar, Juan Perdomo 22, 58, 111
Alexandra Passenger Terminal 115
Allen, Victor 58, 111
American Sugar Company 25
Artus, Frank 20-22, 33, 36, 52, 53
Artus, Mrs. Frank 33
Atlantico Canaria S.A. 118
Autopass Agencies 131
Aznar, Don Eduardo 101
Azores 35

Baez, Marcelo 117, 123
Bahr, Behrend & Co. 101
Baines, Frederick 26
Ballarin y Piera 63
Bennett, Cyril *112*
Bishop, David 111, 128-129, *129*, 130, 131, 132, 135, 138, *142*, 145
Bonny, Antonio 102
Brabyn, Alfred 21, 25, 53, 70, 90
Bradshaw, Harry 89
British Club 47, 53
British Foreign Office 35, 66

Canary Banana Importers 99, 100
Canary Fruit Department 25
Casa de la Real Advana 20
Casa Yeoward (House of Yeoward) 8, 20-22, 24, 36, 52-55, 57, 65-67, 104-105, *108*, 110, 117-118, 120, 133
Cavendish Fruit Stores 64, 95-96, 99
Cejas, Antonio Hernandez 94
Chilean State Railway Company 62
Clark, William 21, 25, 53-54, 63, 66, 80-81, 90, 94, 104-105, 110
Clausen, Mr. & Mrs. Christian 89
Coronation Naval Review *84*, 85
Covent Garden 8, 94-95, 98, 114
CREP (Regional Confederation for the Export of the Banana) 67, 84, 99
Cromwell, Oliver 5
Cuban National Guard 25

Deed of Partnership of Yeoward Brothers 29

E. & L. Sorsky Ltd. 137, 144
Edificio Alondra 124
Edificio Yeoward 110
Elders & Fyffe 90
Empire Preference 64, 67
ETASA 117
Evans, Bertha 3-7, 81
Exportadores de Tomates de Alicante S.A. 109

Falangists 67
FAST 117
Fastnet 38
Fisher, Frederick Edward 8, 19, 36, 58
Fisher, George 95, *112*
Fisher, Harry 58
Five Star Gran Lujo 121
Frith, Arthur *79*
Fyffes 24, 66, 90, 93, 99

G. A. Shipping Ltd. 138
Gallardo, Felix 118, 121
Gaspart, Juan 118
German Naval Staff 35
Gibraltar 71-72, 76, 79
Gil, Adolfo Mathias 118
Gill, Ron 128-129, *129*, 131, 132, *142*, 145
Glaize Brothers of Virginia 26
Glass's Fruit Markets Ltd. 99
González, Luis Herreros 54
Green & Yeoward (Fruit Wholesalers) 1
Green Fruit Department 25
Griffin Travel 115, 131

H. H. Hughes Shipping Ltd. 137
Harvey Buildings *19*, 39
Haywood Shipping Ltd. 137
Hennessey, Jack *111, 112, 114*
Henson, Fred 96
Herederos de R. J. Yeoward 70
Hodgson Morris & Co. 2
Holt, Malcolm 132-133, 135, *142*, 143-145

index

Horesa 118
Hotasa 122
Hotel Botanico *107*, 118-119, 121-125, 134, *141*
Hughes, Brian 131
Hughes, Terry 131, 143
Hull 70, 94, 96, 114
Humphreys, Robert 58
Hunter Travel Services Ltd. 115

Intercon S.A. 109, 121, 123-124, 134
International Astrophysical Observatory 124

J. Jupp & Co. Ltd. 144
J. Koekoek & Co. 94
John Holt & Co. 40
Jones, Alfred 4
Jones, Edward 25
Jones, Geoff 94-100, *97, 111, 112, 114*, 114-115, 129-130, 131

Kaiser Wilhelm Gesellshaft 34
King Juan Carlos 124-125, *126*, 127
Köhler, Herr Doktor Wolfgang 34, 36

Lime Street Square, London, 1, 2
Lopera, Antonio 122

Mark Revill (Liverpool) Ltd. 114
Markads Ltd 100, 124
Mason, Harold 111
Medallo al Merito en el Trabajo 120
Mersey Travelworld 135
Ministry of Food 90, 93
Ministry of War Transport 82, 93
Morell, Enrique 109
Morley, Jim 93, *112, 114*

Naval Authorities 30

Owens, Rex 111, *111, 112*

Pacific Steam Navigation Co. 61
Parque Avoceta 124, 134
Parry, Vic *114*, 131
Pedder, John 2
Pension Fund 32
Placa de Plata de la Orden del Merito Turistico 121
Port of Liverpool Authority 115
Port of Liverpool Fruit Terminal Co. Ltd. 115
Princes Landing Stage 50
Profit Sharing Scheme 114, 129
Prussian Academy of Science 34

Queen Elizabeth II 124, 128
Queen Sofia 124-125, *126*

R. M. Brooker Ltd. 119, 122, 124, 134
R. Wrigglesworth & Son Ltd. 99, 114
Richard J. Yeoward 37
Rio Tinto Co. 32
Royal National Lifeboat Institution (RNLI) 83
Royal Nautical Club 50
Royle, John 99, 102, *112*
Rumasa 121, 122

Salisbury, Ralph 102, *112*
San Sebastian 64
Shipley, William 70, 110-111
Ships
  Aderno 80
  Aguila 13, *15*, 16-18, 26, 29-32, *39*, 39-42, *43*, 48-49, *56, 69*, 69-72, *72, 73*, 74-76, 83
  Aguila Wren 83
  Alca 32, *41*, 41-42, 45, 48-49, 61-62, 70-72, *71*, 78, *79*, 84-86, *85*, 88, 93, 102
  Alfred Jones 77
  Alondra 32, 35, 38, 41-42, *45*, 48, 62
  Alva 74
  Andorinha 13, *16*, 16-18, *17, 18, 21, 23*, 39-40, 57-58, 61
  Ardeola 10, *12, 13*, 13-14, *16*, 16-18, 24, 39-40, *45*, 48, *52*, 62, 70, 78, 80, 83
  Avetero 10, 17-18, 38, 47
  Avocet 9, 10, *10*, 17-18, 32, 38, 41, 47
  Avoceta 41, *45*, 46-48, *51, 59*, 62, 69-71, 76-78, *77*, 83
  Balmore 40
  Bath 73
  Belgien 40
  Bjorn Clausen 89
  Boniface 86
  Ciscar 74
  Don Hugo 32
  Dorrit Clausen 89
  Drammensen 40
  Egret 9
  Empire Defender 79
  Empire Lea 82
  Empire Oak 75
  Fulmar 9
  Girasol 40
  Golden Comet 102
  HMS Leith 72
  HMS Springbank 78
  HMS Zinnia 75
  Lady Plymouth 31
  Lorry 23
  Manchester Vanguard 89
  Manchester Venture 89
  Mirjam 40

Monte Anaga 102, 115
Monte Arucas 101, 103
Monte de la Esperanza 100
Monte Granada 116, *116*, 119
Monte Toledo 116, 119
Monte Ulia 115, 136-137
Monte Umbe 103, *103*, 114, 115, 116
Monte Urquiola 114, 115, *115*
North Wind 131
Orontes 80
Petridge 40
Prominent 89
Ricardo José 23
Scotian 32
Silver Comet 102
Slesvig 82
Starling 77
Stefanie 20
Tadonna 78-79
Titanic 29
Torbay 80
Valdes 38
Verna Clausen 89
Vimy 76
West Wind 131
Yeoward 9
Simpson, George 26, 81, 84, 93, 97, *97*, 99-100, 102, *112*, 129
Simpson, Keppel 130, *142*, 145
Sindical Exportabana S.A. 65
Smith, Maurice 19-20, 36
Spanish Minister of Tourism 121

Tabrett, Arthur 124, 133

Terry Brothers 26
Travellers Consultant Services Ltd. 119
Treaty of Montreal 64
Trust Deed 39

Victoria Street 1, 25, 7, 115

Wardle, Joseph P. 61, 69, 81, 90
Weightman Pedder & Co. 2, 21
Weightman Rutherfords 2

Yeoward & Co. (Shipbrokers) 1, 2
Yeoward Brothers (Tankers) Ltd 132
Yeoward Brothers 1, 3-4, 8, 18, 21-22, 25-26, 37, 40, 61, 66, 70, 80, 82-83, 89-90, 94, 96-97
Yeoward Brothers Deterioration Clause 26
Yeoward Brothers Ltd. 97, 100-103, 105, 111, 114, 117, 119, 129-131
Yeoward Group 131-133, 136-138, 143-145
Yeoward Hermanos 8
Yeoward Real Estat S.r.l. 95-96
Yeoward Superannuation Fund 39, 98, 111
Yeoward, Bernard Evans 29, 37, 61, 104-106, 123
Yeoward, Cyril 29, 37
Yeoward, Evaline 62, 104-106, 111
Yeoward, Ida Evans 36
Yeoward, Joseph 2
Yeoward, Mylou 124, *139*
Yeoward, Rosemary 130, *142*, 145
Yeoward, Virginia 130, 143, 145
Yeoward, William 2